BREAKING AND ENTERING

STUDIES IN CRIME, LAW AND JUSTICE

Series Editor: James A. Inciardi,
Division of Criminal Justice, University of Delaware

Studies in Crime, Law and Justice contains original research formulations and new analytic perspectives on continuing important issues of crime and the criminal justice and legal systems. Volumes are research based but are written in nontechnical language to allow for use in courses in criminal justice, criminology, law, social problems, and related subjects.

Studies are both contributions to the research literature and ideal text supplements, and are of interest to academics, professionals, and students.

BREAKING AND ENTERING
An Ethnographic Analysis of Burglary

BY

Paul F. Cromwell
University of Miami

James N. Olson and D'Aunn Wester Avary
The University of Texas—Permian Basin

This research was supported by National Institute of Justice
grant No. 88-IJ-CX-0042. The opinions expressed are those of
the authors and do not necessarily represent the position or
policies of the United States Department of Justice.

STUDIES IN CRIME, LAW, AND JUSTICE ■ Volume 8

SAGE PUBLICATIONS
The International Professional Publishers
Newbury Park London New Delhi

For information address:

SAGE Publications, Inc.
2455 Teller Road
Newbury Park, California 91320

SAGE Publications Ltd.
6 Bonhill Street
London EC2A 4PU
United Kingdom

SAGE Publications India Pvt. Ltd.
M-32 Market
Greater Kailash I
New Delhi 110 048 India

Printed in the United States of America

Library of Congress Cataloging-in-Publication Data

Cromwell, Paul F.
    Breaking and entering : an ethnographic analysis of burglary / by
Paul F. Cromwell and James N. Olson and D'Aunn W. Avary.
        p.   cm. — (Studies in crime, law, and justice)
    Includes bibliographical references.
    ISBN 0-8039-4026-2. — ISBN 0-8039-4027-0
    1. Burglary—United States. I. Olson, James N. II. Avary,
D'Aunn W. (D'Aunn Wester) III. Title. IV. Series.
HV6658.C77   1991
364.1′62—dc20   90-21366
                                                          CIP

FIRST PRINTING, 1991

Sage Production Editor: Judith L. Hunter

Contents

To Christopher Cromwell, Rebecca Cromwell, Karen Cromwell, Katheryn Cromwell, Travis Olson, and Morgan Avary.

Acknowledgments

We take this opportunity to express our sincere appreciation for the assistance and support of the many persons who aided us in this endeavor. Their contribution to the research was immeasurable.

The encouragement and active assistance of Chief of Police Richard Czech and Lt. Jerry Morris of the Midland (Texas) Police Department, Sheriff Gary Painter and Lt. Tim Rogers of the Midland County Sheriff's Department, District Attorney Al Schorre, Chief Adult Probation Officer George W. Thompson, and Adult Probation Officer Diane Deramus were key to the success of the project.

The inspiration for this study was the pioneering work of Professors C. Ray Jeffery, Paul and Patricia Brantingham, Neal Shover, Ronald Clarke, Marcus Felson, Ronald Hunter, and other "environmental criminologists." In addition to encouragement and inspiration, we received advice (not always taken) and helpful counsel from them. To them goes much of the credit for the success of this study; however, the errors are ours alone. We are indebted to each of them.

Our statistical consultants, Alan Marks and Kenneth Pfeiffer, were patient and long-suffering. We express our special appreciation to them.

Jimmie Cromwell tirelessly transcribed tapes of the interviews and edited the final version of the report. Hers was a Herculean effort. Angela Crick, Senior Secretary in the Division of Behavioral Sciences, and graduate assistants Sandra Wester and Carla Curtner performed "above and beyond," keeping the project on schedule and running smoothly.

We are also grateful for the guidance and support we received from Ms. Winifred Reed, Program Manager at the National Institute of Justice, which funded the research. We also received much encouragement and assistance from the NIJ project monitors; R. Gil Kerlikowske, Chief of Police in Fort Pierce, Florida; Albert Reiss; William Graham

Sumner, Professor of Sociology at Yale University; and Carl Klockars, Professor of Sociology at the University of Delaware.

Finally, we must acknowledge our debt to the subjects of this study. These persons gave us their trust and provided us with insights we could never have obtained otherwise. Although they remain forever anonymous, we are grateful for their assistance.

Paul F. Cromwell
James N. Olson
D'Aunn W. Avary

1

Environmental Criminology, Rationality, and Crime

Much of the recent research in environmental criminology, particularly crime-specific studies (Åkerström, 1983; Bennett & Wright, 1984; Brown & Altman, 1981; Nee & Taylor, 1988; Reppetto, 1974; Scarr, 1973; Shover, 1971; Wright & Logie, 1988) has focused on the rational processes by which an offender chooses a criminal career, selects targets, and carries out criminal acts. Rational choice theory is predicated on the assumption that individuals choose to commit crimes. Rational choice theory predicts that individuals evaluate alternative courses of action, weighing the possible rewards against the costs and risks, and choosing the action that maximizes their gain.

The notion of rational choice has its origins in both the classical theories of Cesare Beccaria and Jeremy Bentham in the late eighteenth century and in relatively recent economic theory. According to classical theory criminals are free, rational, and hedonistic. They choose among alternative courses of action according to their perceptions of the risks and gains associated, seeking to maximize gain (or pleasure) and minimize risk (or pain). Because they exercise free will in choosing among alternatives, they are responsible for their actions (Barlow, 1990). Modern classical explanations are derived from economic theory, which views the decision to commit crime as essentially like any other decision—that is, one made on the basis of a calculation of the costs and benefits of the action (Vold & Bernard, 1986). The benefits of a criminal action are the net rewards of crime and include not only the material

This research was supported by National Institute of Justice Grant No. 88-IJ-CX-0042. The opinions expressed are those of the authors and do not necessarily represent the position or policies of the United States Department of Justice.

gains but also intangible benefits such as emotional satisfactions. The individual may receive immense satisfaction from the excitement of crime, from the independent life-style afforded by crime, or from outwitting the authorities. The risks or costs of crime are those associated with formal punishment should the individual be discovered, apprehended, and convicted, as well as psychological or social costs, such as pangs of conscience, social disapproval, marital and family discord, or loss of self-esteem (Vold & Bernard, 1986).

The degree of rationality that can be attributed to offenders in planning and executing their crimes and how rationality is related to crime prevention measures have been central issues of debate (Clarke & Cornish, 1985; Cook, 1980). One approach suggests that criminal decision making is highly rational, following a sequential, hierarchical course from the decision to offend to the selection of the actual target (Brantingham & Brantingham, 1978; Brown & Altman, 1981). These models have characteristics of flowchart diagrams or decision trees, identifying the main decision points and the factors bearing on the decisions made at each step. Researchers in this tradition contemplate an offender who has formed a mental template or a cognitive map of an area, and reached a decision to offend on the basis of the fit between the crime situation and the template or cognitive map. Studies by Shover (1971), Reppetto (1974), Walsh (1980), and Bennett and Wright (1984) have generally supported this model.

Others propose a more limited view of rationality (Clarke & Cornish, 1985; Cook, 1980). For behavior to be rational, it does not have to be carefully preconceived and planned or require hierarchical, sequential decision making. It is enough that decisions are perceived to be optimal. This view of rationality does not require deliberate weighing of carefully considered alternatives and consequences. It is sufficient that decision makers choose between alternatives based upon their immediate perception of the risks and gains involved. The decision does not have to be the best possible under the circumstances, nor does it have to be based upon an accurate assessment of the situation. And, as Wilson and Herrnstein (1985) conclude, the value of any reward or punishment associated with a criminal action is always uncertain. A burglar can never calculate with assurance the value of the property he or she expects to take away in a burglary or know with confidence the extent of the punishment should he or she be apprehended.

The concept of *limited rationality* recognizes the limited capacity and willingness of most persons to acquire and process information from more than one input or source simultaneously. Cornish and Clarke (1986) concluded that people usually pay attention to only some of the facts or sources at their disposal, employing shortcuts or rules of thumb to speed the decision process. These rules of thumb are analogous to Cook's (1980) concept of *standing decisions,* which negate the need to weigh carefully all the alternatives and consequences before making a decision in many cases. A standing decision may simply be a decision made beforehand to take advantage of certain types of criminal opportunities or to avoid others. None of this, however, implies irrationality. Rational choice theories need only presume that some minimal degree of planning and foresight occurs (Hirschi, 1985).

One limited rationality approach views criminal decision making as primarily a product of opportunity (Cohen & Felson, 1979; Rengert & Wasilchick, 1985; Scarr, 1973). In a study of burglary in Washington, D.C., Scarr (1973) concluded that the majority of burglaries were the result of exploitation of opportunity rather than careful, rational planning. Offenders develop a sensitivity to the opportunities in everyday life for illicit gain. This position assumes that burglars and other motivated individuals see criminal opportunity in situations where others might not. This "alert opportunism" (Shover, 1971), or "criminal mind" as our informants labeled the phenomenon, allows them to recognize rapidly and take advantage of potential criminal opportunities.[1] Their unique perspective toward the world results from learning experiences that have sensitized them to events that are ignored by most. Just as a carpenter looking at a house notes the quality of workmanship and other characteristics that are salient to him or her because of his or her profession, burglars assess the possibility of gain versus the potential risk involved in burglarizing a site. They do not simply see an open window, but rather the potential for covert entry and a "fast buck." These processes are almost automatic and are as much a part of the tools of the burglar as a pry bar or a window jimmy.

Opportunity models are not necessarily inconsistent with rational choice explanations of criminal decision making. The essential element of rational choice theory is that offenders freely and actively choose to commit crimes and make decisions based upon an analysis of the risks and gains implicit in the proposed act. The decisions do not have to be the best under the circumstances. They must only be perceived by the decision maker to have been made after rational calculation.

If the rational model of behavior has value in analyzing criminal behavior, it should be reflected in the selection of targets by criminals, especially burglars. Burglary is an instrumental crime almost always committed to fulfill economic needs. Unlike expressive crimes, which are done for their own sake, burglary should be a model of rational choice behavior.

Some environmental criminologists (Bennett & Wright, 1984; Brantingham & Brantingham, 1978, 1981; Brown & Altman, 1981) have focused on the burglar's use of distinctive environmental stimuli that function as signals or cues to provide salient information about the environment's temporal, spatial, socio-cultural, psychological, and legal characteristics. An individual who is motivated to commit a crime uses these discriminative cues to locate and identify target sites. With practice the individual gains experience and learns which discriminative cues and which combination or sequence of cues are associated with "good" targets. These cues are "a template which is used in victim or target selection. Potential victims or targets are compared to the template and either rejected or accepted, depending on the congruence" (Brantingham & Brantingham, 1978, p. 108). In effect, these are standing decisions that do not require conscious analysis each time they are employed. Regardless of whether the individual is consciously aware of the construction and implementation of the template, each time it is successfully employed it is reinforced and becomes relatively automatic. Although the template may become the primary decision-making tool of the burglar, he or she may not be able to articulate the underlying processing strategies or the discriminative cues or cue clusters that guide the target selection process. He or she may accept or reject a potential crime site based upon its fit with a mental template constructed and applied without conscious awareness.

There have been suggestions that altered states of arousal and disequilibrium (such as inebriation or symptoms of drug withdrawal) may inhibit, distort, or in some way short-circuit the normal decision-making processes during states of equilibrium (Brantingham & Brantingham, 1978; Brown & Altman, 1981). Although most would probably agree that altered states of arousal have the potential to disrupt the normal decision-making process, no one appears to have addressed the issue beyond acknowledging that differences may exist in the decision-making process within the same individual depending upon the state of disequilibrium or state of arousal. Brown and Altman (1981), for instance, state that although they recognize the possibility of an affectively motivated burglar (one who is highly aroused) not attending to social or environmental cues, such a situation would conflict with their sequential model. Consequently, they restrict their model to experienced, professional, instrumentally motivated burglars.

PURPOSE

The present research is a study of burglars and burglary. It is concerned with how offenders go about their business; the kinds of things they do or fail to do before and during the commission of a crime. It attempts to understand their perceptions of the risks and rewards involved in criminal activity, particularly in residential property crime. Of particular interest are their perceptions of the sanction threat of the criminal justice system and how those perceptions are formed and evolve, and are modified over time. It is further concerned with how residential burglars select targets, how the presence of co-offenders influences decision-making processes, and how narcotics and drug abuse influence the prevalence and incidence of residential property crime, as well as what role drugs play in target selection and the risk-gain calculus employed by burglars.

One specific purpose of the present study is to determine the extent to which residential burglars utilize rational processes to select burglary targets and what environmental factors are used as discriminative cues in the target selection process.

The second purpose of the study is to determine the effects of drug use on the rational choice decision model. Recent research (Johnson et al., 1985) suggests that as many as two thirds of all burglars are addicted to drugs or have used drugs in the recent past. If drug usage (and concomitant arousal and disequilibrium) affects the rational, sequential decision model of target selection by residential burglars, and if 60% to 70% of all burglars are drug abusers, decision-making models that assume a rational cognitive state are limited in explanatory power, predictive ability, and generalizability.

The third purpose of the research is to determine how or by what processes decision making is modified or changed depending on whether or not the burglar is alone or working with accomplices. The literature in social psychology suggests that decisions made by groups are either more risky or more cautious than initial decisions made by individual members of the same group (Shaw, 1981). There is also evidence to suggest that group affiliation increases the drive level of group members and that performance on tasks requiring creativity or the use of judgment skills is impaired by the presence of coactors (Allport, 1920; Shaw, 1981; Zajonc, 1965, 1980). This suggests that burglars working with co-offenders may have a higher rate of offending than burglars working alone, and that they might experience impairment in their performance.

The fourth purpose of the study is to evaluate marketing or "fencing" strategies for stolen property as a corollary to burglary. Although there are several excellent studies of the professional fence (Klockars, 1974; Steffensmeier, 1986), there is little research on other avenues for the marketing of stolen property (see Henry, 1978). The present study assesses behavior of criminal receivers of stolen property and attempts to describe the less well-known avenues of fencing stolen goods by burglars.

The final purpose of the study is to assess to what extent the criminal justice system deters the residential burglar from initiating or continuing in a criminal career.

METHOD

Thirty active burglars in an urban Texas metropolitan area of 250,000 population were recruited as research subjects (hereinafter referred to as informants) using a snowball sampling procedure. Three informants were recruited initially by referral from local criminal justice agencies. They were promised complete confidentiality, anonymity, and a stipend of $50 for each active burglar referred by them and accepted for the study. The additional informants thus recruited were also promised confidentiality, anonymity, and a stipend of $50 for every interview, as well as an additional stipend for each additional, new active burglar they recruited. Informants who usually worked with partners (co-offenders) were encouraged to recruit their co-offenders. The initial three informants, who had worked with the researchers for a year during a pilot study, vouched for the researchers and verified the nature of the research to those persons they recruited, who in turn did the same for those they referred.

Potential informants were screened to determine their qualifications. A potential informant was eligible to participate in the study if he or she admitted committing a minimum of two burglaries per month *and* satisfied two or more of the following requirements: (a) had been convicted by the courts or labeled by the police as a burglar, (b) perceived

Table 1.1 Characteristics of Burglars

	Frequency According to Ethnicity, Gender, and Drug of Choice.						
	White		*Hispanic*		*Black*		
Drug of choice	*male*	*female*	*male*	*female*	*male*	*female*	*Total*
Heroin	4	2	3	1	2	—	12
Cocaine	2	—	4	—	5	—	11
Alcohol	—	—	1	—	—	—	1
Marijuana	1	—	—	—	3	—	4
Methamphetamine (speed)	1	—	—	—	1	—	2
Total	8	2	8	1	11	0	30

and labeled himself or herself as a burglar, and (c) was perceived or labeled by peers as a burglar.[2] Four informants who had recently desisted—quit active burglary—were included in the sample (see discussion in Appendix A).

The final sample was composed of 27 males and 3 females and was nearly evenly distributed among white, Hispanic, and black burglars. The mean age was 25 years; the range was 16 to 43 years. All of the burglars were drug addicts or abusers of illegal drugs. Table 1.1 presents the sample by drug of choice, gender, and ethnicity.

Staged Activity Analysis

There are two generally accepted methods for the collection of data within an ethnographic design: (a) direct participant observation and (b) the ethnographic interview (Glassner & Carpenter, 1985). Entering the burglars' world as a participant and observing their behavior from that vantage point would provide insights that could not be gained through other research strategies. Legal and ethical problems, however, generally preclude such an approach. On the other hand, ethnographic interviews with criminal subjects about their own criminal behavior frequently produce misleading results.

We selected an alternative strategy: one that we termed *staged activity analysis*.[3] The subjects were asked to reconstruct and simulate their past burglaries as nearly as possible in the same manner in which they were originally committed. The researcher observed, questioned, and recorded the events and answers. No crimes were committed by either the subjects or the researchers. Most legal and ethical problems involved in conducting the research were eliminated through this technique (see Appendix A for a more detailed account of the legal and ethical problems considered).

Staged activity analysis consists of extensive interviews and "ride alongs," during which the informants were asked to discuss and evaluate residential sites they had previously burglarized and sites previously burglarized by other informants in the study. Each informant participated in as many as nine sessions with the researchers.

Session 1 consisted of a semistructured interview three to four hours in duration. During this session the informant was asked a series of open-ended questions ranging from queries about how he or she began as a burglar to specific questions about cues, motivations, probing strategies (casing), and disposing (fencing) of stolen goods. The remaining eight sessions involved actual visits to sites previously burglarized by the informant and other informants in the study. Sessions were conducted under all conditions in which burglars might conceivably commit their crimes: in the daytime, at night, with an informant alone, with informants grouped with their usual co-offenders, when using drugs, when stable, and when needing a drug administration (withdrawing). Before each session the informants were asked to estimate their own drug state at the time of the session and to recall their drug state at the time of the actual burglary of the site. An informant's drug state was estimated as follows:

(1) *Nonuser;*
(2) *Aroused:* in need of a drug administration (sick or in the early stages of withdrawal);
(3) *Regular user/stable:* having administered a drug recently and in no immediate need of another drug administration;
(4) *Regular user/high:* having administered a drug recently and feeling intoxicated, stoned, high, or nodding off;
(5) *Intermittent user/stable:* no drugs in the past 12 hours and no immediate need for drugs;
(6) *Intermittent user/high:* not a regular user but having administered a drug recently and feeling intoxicated, stoned, high, or nodding off.

Session 2 was a daytime visit to at least one site previously burglarized ("hit") by the informant and to sites recently burglarized by others.[4] The informants were then asked to direct the interviewer to the site of a recent burglary, using the method of travel and route taken at the time of the actual burglary. The informants were asked to recall why they had chosen that specific route and neighborhood or area of the city.

Upon arriving in the general neighborhood of the target site the informants were instructed to proceed to the target site in as nearly as possible the same manner as they had at the time of the actual burglary. At the target site, the informants were asked a series of open-ended questions relating to the burglary, with emphasis on salient and subtle cues relied upon to select the target, including cues relating to occupancy, potential gain, and perceived risks. The informants were also queried about probes used to determine occupancy, method of entry, techniques of searching, division of labor (if co-offenders were involved), what was taken, the route and method of escape, how the stolen property was converted to cash or drugs, and how any money obtained by disposing of the stolen property was spent. Open-ended questions were pursued in detail depending upon the informants' willingness and ability to discuss each specific topic.

Following the interview, informants were asked to drive or walk through the immediate neighborhood and select a residence that they considered a *high risk* site, that is, one that they were very unlikely to burglarize. After this selection the informants were asked why they rejected the high risk site and what would need to be different in order to consider the site a good target for burglary.

Each informant was then driven to at least two sites previously burglarized by other informants and to at least two sites selected by other informants as high risk. At each previously burglarized site and its matched high risk site, the informant was asked to rate the site in terms of its vulnerability and attractiveness as an *immediate* burglary target given the circumstances that prevailed at the time of the staged activity analysis. The sites were rated on a scale of 0 to 10. An *attractiveness rating* of zero meant, "Under the circumstances that are present now, I would not burglarize this residence." A rating of 10 meant, "This is a very attractive and vulnerable target and I would definitely take steps to burglarize it *right now.*" In addition, each informant was presented with two hypothetical situations and asked to provide an attractiveness rating for each: (1) If you knew no one was at home at this residence, what rating would you give the site on attractiveness as a burglary target *right now;* and (2) if you knew no one was home and you knew that there was $250 in cash inside, what rating would you give the residence on its attractiveness as a burglary target *right now?*

Thus Session 2 consisted of evaluating at least two previously burglarized sites and at least two sites selected by informants as high risk. All Session 2 sites were evaluated during daylight hours.

Session 3 was conducted in essentially the same manner, except that it was a group session. The informant was grouped with his or her co-offenders, if any.[5] The purpose of this session was to determine to what extent, if any, group decisions differed from individual decisions. During group sessions the informants were asked to provide individual attractiveness ratings of the various sites without discussion with their co-offender(s). The informants were then encouraged to discuss the target site with their co-offender(s) and arrive at a group attractiveness rating. The drug state of each member was determined prior to evaluating the sites.

Session 4 took place at night. The informants evaluated sites they had previously burglarized at night (if any) and sites burglarized by others at night, along with their matched high risk counterparts.

Session 5 was a group night session. Session 6 was an individual day session. Session 7 was a group day session. Session 8 was an individual night (and debriefing) session and Session 9 was a group night (and debriefing) session. All sessions followed the same format as Sessions 1 through 4.

At the conclusion of Session 9 informants had evaluated up to 21 previously burglarized sites and their matched high risk counterparts. Informants who never worked with partners and those whose partners refused to cooperate did not participate in Session 3, 5, and 9, and informants who burglarized only in the daytime did not participate in night sessions and vice versa. Three hundred and ten session hours with 30 active burglars were conducted. Each session was tape-recorded and verbatim transcripts were made.

Two quantitative substudies were conducted to validate partially the ethnographic data obtained from the burglar informants. One consisted of comparing 300 burglarized residences to 300 nonburglarized residences. The burglarized residences were obtained by selecting every *n*th case from the records of burglaries reported to the local police during 1987 and 1988. The nonburglarized residences were selected by taking every *n*th residential building from the city tax rolls. The tax roll residences were screened by comparing them to 1987 and 1988 burglary reports. Residences that reported burglaries during 1987 and 1988 were eliminated until 300 residences with no reported burglaries for the two-year period were obtained.[6]

Each burglarized and nonburglarized residence was evaluated in terms of its attributes on the following variables: distance from corner, distance from stop sign, distance from traffic light, distance from school, distance from commercial business establishment, distance from park, distance from church, distance to nearest four-lane street, number of lanes of traffic in front of residence, average speed of traffic in front of residence, and presence or absence of garage or carport. A discriminant analysis was performed to determine which variables best discriminated between the burglarized and nonburglarized residences.

The second quantitative substudy compared the evaluations of previously burglarized and high risk sites by burglars to those of a control group of noncriminals. Twenty-eight student controls were asked to rate 20 sites that had previously been rated by the burglar informants. The mean age of the control subjects was 25 and ranged from 18 to 48 years. At each previously burglarized site and its matched high risk site, the controls were asked to rate the site in terms of its vulnerability and attractiveness as a burglary target. The sites were rated on the same scale as that used by the burglar informants. The ratings of the control group were compared to those of the burglar informants to determine whether naive raters and burglars differed in their evaluation of a potential burglary target.

2

The Burglary Event

A considerable body of literature has examined the specific content of the cues utilized by burglars in the target selection process, and the specific techniques employed by burglars in the actual burglary (Åkerström, 1983; Bennett & Wright, 1984; Brown & Altman, 1981; Nee & Taylor, 1988; Rengert & Wasilchick, 1985; Reppetto, 1974; Scarr, 1973; Shover, 1971; Wright & Logie, 1988). The conclusions are consistent in relation to some factors, but not in relation to others.

MOTIVATION

The motivation that drives the burglary event is a consistent factor. Bennett and Wright (1984, p. 31) found that burglars' motivations fell into six major categories, listed here in order of importance:

(1) instrumental needs,
(2) influence of others,
(3) influence of presented opportunities,
(4) none (the individual is constantly motivated),
(5) expressive needs, and
(6) alcohol.

Scarr (1973) found that burglars in his study cited, in order of importance, the following motivations:

(1) need for money to buy drugs,
(2) need for money to lead a "fast expensive life,"

(3) social motives (gangs, delinquent subcultures, peer approval, status), and
(4) idiosyncratic motives (kicks, thrills, pathological behavior, rebellion).

Reppetto's (1974) subjects reported satisfaction of their need for money as the primary motivation for their robberies and burglaries. Subsidiary satisfactions such as excitement, revenge, and curiosity were cited by a significant but smaller percentage of the subjects. Excitement as a motive was mentioned most often by the younger burglars and less often by the older. Only 10% of Reppetto's subjects stated that they would continue to commit burglary if their need for money, including money for drugs, was satisfied (p. 22).

Rengert and Wasilchick (1985) concluded, "The primary reason stated by burglars we interviewed for deciding to commit a burglary was simply to obtain money. . . . The need for money arose out of psychologically defined needs, not subsistence needs" (p. 54).

Our findings were consistent with Rengert and Wasilchick's (1985), with those of Scarr (1973), and to a lesser extent with those of Reppetto (1974). Informants stressed need for money to fulfill expressive needs as the primary motivation for their criminal behavior. Only one informant reported a primary need for money to purchase something other than alcohol or drugs or for "partying." He used burglary proceeds primarily to support his gambling habit. Although virtually every burglar used some of his or her proceeds to buy food and clothing, and to pay for shelter, transportation, and other licit needs, the greatest percentage of the proceeds from burglary went toward the purchase of drugs and alcohol and for the activity they loosely labeled as partying.

Second in importance was the need for money to maintain a "fast, expensive life." Keeping up appearances was stressed by many as a critical concern. This was especially true for black burglars. One informant summed up the attitude of black burglars this way:

You gotta understand about blacks. It's important to keep up a front, to have money and for people to know you have money. Looking good is important. You can't get women if you don't have some bread.

Excitement and thrills were mentioned by almost every informant; however, only a few would commit a burglary for that purpose only. Like Reppetto, we concluded that the younger, less experienced burglars were more prone to commit crimes for the thrill and excitement.

Many burglars, however, reported that they had in the past committed a burglary for the excitement only.

About 30% of the informants reported committing at least one burglary for revenge. They seldom obtained much material reward in revenge burglaries, reporting instead that they "trashed" the victim's house. This tendency was more pronounced among burglars under 25 years of age. One burglar told the interviewer:

I was helping this friend move into a new house and the white lady next door saw that we were black. I heard her tell another neighbor that she was upset about a black man moving in next door. I decided to come back the next day and "do" her house for revenge.

Another said that he had burglarized the house of a former friend after that individual had "snitched" on him. He said:

I didn't take nothing except some food. Mainly I just trashed his place. I was really pissed off.

TIME OF BURGLARY

Rengert and Wasilchick (1985), in a study of use of time by residential burglars, found that the time patterns of burglars are determined by the time patterns of their victims. Burglars work during periods when residences are left unguarded. They concluded that if a home is guarded (occupied) during the day, it is likely to be guarded by women. Rengert and Wasilchick (1985) state that women who do not work outside the home tend to develop predictable patterns regarding the use of discretionary time for the purpose of shopping, errands, or visiting friends and relatives. Women who work outside the home develop similar patterns of time use on Saturday and Sunday. In either case, the use of discretionary time for the purpose of shopping and running errands is observable and predictable by residential burglars. Whenever the house is left unguarded, it is susceptible to burglary. They wrote: "When we combine the daily activities of many women, we can identify times when the typical house is not likely to be guarded" (Rengert & Wasilchick, 1985, p. 26).

They found burglars to be most active between 10:00 and 11:00 a.m. and from 1:00 to 3:00 p.m. Our informants stated they preferred to work

Table 2.1 Day Versus Night Burglary Ratings

Time	At present (now)	Hypothetical Circumstances	
		Assuming no one is home	Assuming no one is home and $250 cash is inside
Day	3.52 (126)	4.97 (105)	5.88 (91)
Night	2.26 (117)	5.44 (108)	6.55 (107)
	$F(1,203) = 11.36$	$F(1,173) = 0.36$	$F(1,158) = 2.00$
	$p < .05$	$p > .05$	$p > .05$

The individual burglary attractiveness ratings (means) of burglars alone under the circumstances that actually prevailed at the time of the site inspection (now) and hypothetical circumstances for day and night staged analyses. The number of individual ratings from which each mean was obtained is given in parentheses. The results of two-sample tests comparing day and night means are given below.

between 9:00 and 11:00 a.m. and in mid-afternoon. Most organized their working hours around school hours, particularly during the times when parents (usually mothers) took children to school and picked them up after school. Several told us that they waited "until the wife left to take the kids to school or go shopping." Most stated that they did not do burglaries on Saturday because people were usually home then. However, Sunday morning during church hours was considered prime time for weekend burglary.

Only a small number ($n = 3$) of burglars in our study committed burglaries at night. Most preferred to commit their crimes during hours when they expected people to be at work and out of the home. As seen in Table 2.1, during the staged activity analysis informants rated targets more attractive and more vulnerable when they were rated during daylight hours than when the same targets were rated at night. However, the day versus night variation was not significant under the hypothetical circumstances in which the informants were asked to assume that no one was home, and to assume that no one was home and $250 in cash was inside. In the hypothetical situations the critical variable of occupancy was established (no one is home) and the variation across raters was essentially washed out. The lack of statistical significance under these circumstances is not, therefore, attributable to day versus night variations but rather to the issue of occupancy.

Those who did commit nighttime burglary usually knew the victims and their schedules or took advantage of people being away from home in the evening during special events, such as high school football games. Pep squads at the high schools in the area studied decorate the front yards of the football team members with signs that identify the player, position, and uniform number. Burglars told us that they knew these houses would most likely be empty on Friday nights because the families attended the game. One said:

Man! Wait until football season. I clean up then. When they are at the game, I'm at their house.

The typical burglar is much more aware of our use of time than we are. As Rengert and Wasilchick (1985, p.52) conclude, "We are all waiting to become victims of a burglar whose intuition about time coincides with our routine."

OCCUPANCY PROBES

Almost all burglars avoid selecting as targets houses that are occupied. Over 90% of our informants stated that they would never enter a residence that they knew was occupied. Therefore, it is important that the burglar develop techniques to probe the potential target site to determine if anyone is at home. There are various ways, some quite ingenious, in which burglars probe the target to determine occupancy. These occupancy probes are quite similar across studies. This may be the result of simple common sense, or it may result from sharing of techniques by burglars on street corners, in bars, and in prisons and jails.

The most common probe used by our informants was to send one of the burglars, usually the most presentable (or the woman), to the door to knock or ring the doorbell. If someone answered the prober would ask directions to a nearby address or for a nonexistent person, for example, "Is Ray home?" The prospective burglar would apologize and leave when told that he or she had the wrong address. Burglars also occasionally ring the doorbell and ask the resident for use of the phone: "My car broke down across the street. May I use your phone to call a garage?" This is a good strategy. If the resident refuses, the prober can leave without arousing suspicion. If, however, the resident agrees, the prober has the additional opportunity to assess the quality and quantity of the potential take and to learn more about the security, location of windows and doors, dogs, alarms, and so forth. Several who used this strategy reported that they usually raised the hood of their car or removed a tire in order to give their story legitimacy. Rengert and Wasilchick (1985) reported similar strategies: "One of our burglars likes to pretend to have car problems. He would turn into a driveway of a likely house and raise the hood of his car. If the doorbell was answered, he asked for water for his overheated radiator" (p. 89).

Several informants reported obtaining the resident's name from the mailbox or from a sign over the door. They would then look up the telephone number and call the residence, leaving the phone ringing while they returned to the target home. If they could still hear the phone ringing when they arrived back at the house, they were sure that the house was unoccupied. This technique suggests that home owners should *not* place their name anywhere outside their home. This gives the burglar the information needed (name and address) to look up the telephone number.

Some burglars, particularly the more professional, will probe neighbors next door to, and across the street from, the target. The ideal target is one where no one is home adjacent to and in houses overlooking the target. One burglar informant chose houses next door to homes that exhibited a "For Sale" sign. She would dress and act like a potential buyer, walking around the yard of the for-sale home, peering in windows, and so on, finally entering the backyard of the for-sale home and from there climbing the adjoining fence into the backyard of the target home.

Some burglars watch a target home until they see the occupants leave for work in the morning; after a quick probe for a remaining occupant, they enter the house. One informant drives around residential neighborhoods until he sees a resident leaving. He enters after a quick probe for remaining occupants.

One informant in the study dressed in jogging gear and removed a piece of mail from the potential target house mailbox. He then knocked on the door and if the resident answered, he told them he had found the piece of mail in the street and was returning it. The jogging gear gave him legitimacy in a strange neighborhood, and returning the mail made him appear to be a good citizen. Thus he aroused no suspicions.

Another informant, a female heroin addict, carried her two-year-old child to the target residence door, asking for directions to a nearby address. While at the door she would ask for a "drink of water for the baby." She reported that even those who appeared suspicious seldom denied her entry to get the baby a drink.

TECHNIQUES FOR ENTRY

One of the skills that separates the novice burglar from the journey-man and the professional is his or her skill at covert entry (breaking in). The break-in techniques, like the occupancy probes, were generally similar across studies. There were occasional unusual and creative methods, however, the skills appeared to be generic. One of our inform-ants, among the most skilled of all the subjects in the study, was employed for a period of time by a glass repair and replacement company. He could remove a pane of glass in less than a minute and replace it when he left. He stated:

I always put the pane back in and I don't disturb anything in the house. Sometimes the burglary doesn't even get reported. If I take small stuff, like jewelry, sometimes the people don't even miss it for a week or two and when they do, they think they lost it or something.

A popular way of entering a residence is through sliding glass patio doors. These doors may be popped out of their sliding tracks by hand or with the aid of a crowbar or screwdriver. Entry is quick and noiseless. Less skilled burglars insert a screwdriver between the door and the frame, break the usually cheaply built locks, and slide the door open. Some informants considered this method less professional than remov-ing the door completely, although both appear to be quick and noiseless.

Other methods have a substantial number of adherents: (1) The burglar enters through a rear door by forcing the door with a pry tool or by the simple expedient of kicking it down. (2) The burglar enters an open garage door and then forces open the door between the garage and the house. (3) The burglar removes or breaks a window pane and crawls in through the opened window. This is common with the professional, who will often remove the window pane or cut the glass (both are noiseless operations) and then reach in and open the window. Several burglars reported removing window air conditioning units and entering through the resulting opening. Another stated that he had removed skylights and entered through the roof.

Three informants used large channel lock pliers to twist the doorknob off the front door of the residence. This technique works so quickly on most doors that the burglar appears to be using a key to enter.

One petite female burglar was able to crawl through pet doors. Her burglaries stumped law enforcement for a considerable period because there was no evidence of forced entry in her jobs. Another burglar put his three-year-old daughter through pet doors and other small openings. After gaining entry in this manner, she had been taught to open the back door of the house for her father.

Some burglars may simply kick down a door or smash a window with little apparent concern for noise. These are usually heroin addicts who are sick and in desperate need of a fix; cocaine, crack, or amphetamine users who are high; or the least experienced and nonskilled burglars. These measures subject the burglar to a much greater risk of detection and arrest.

INSIDE INFORMATION

Professional burglars often work with "inside men" who have access to potential targets and advise the burglar about things to steal. They may also provide such critical information as times when the owner is away and of weaknesses in security. One female heroin addict maintained close contact with several women who worked as maids in affluent sections of the community. She would gain the necessary information from these women and later come back and break into the house, often entering by a door or window left open for her by the accomplice.

A more common scenario was for the burglar to learn of the habits and activities of home owners from maids, gardeners, and others who had no intention of knowingly assisting a burglar. Friends who worked in these jobs would alert him to possible burglaries through casual talks about their job or their employer, mentioning, for instance, that the family they worked for was leaving for a two-week vacation, or that they had just purchased a new television or VCR. The burglar then used that otherwise innocent information to commit a burglary.

People involved in a variety of service jobs (repair, carpet cleaning, pizza delivery, lawn maintenance, plumbing, carpentry) enter many homes each day and have the opportunity to assess the quality of potential stolen merchandise and security measures taken by the residents. Burglars will often establish contact with employees of these businesses for purposes of obtaining this inside information. One informant said:

I like to date maids. They know who has what and how to get it. I get them to talk about their job and the people they work for and I use that information to do burglaries.

In one case, an employee of a maid service worked closely with a burglar. This maid provided information to the burglar about security, times when the residents were away from home, and a list with specific locations of valuable goods inside the house.

Information about potential targets was frequently gained from fences. Because many fences have legitimate occupations, they may have knowledge of the existence of valuable property from social or business relationships. They can often provide the burglar with information about the owners' schedules and the security arrangements at the target site (see Chapter 6). Pawnshop employees may also be able to provide burglars with information about potential targets. One professional burglar told the interviewer that an employee at a pawnshop provided him with copies of jewelry appraisals and the addresses of potential targets.

Inside knowledge is also obtained by persons who work regularly in a neighborhood but who never actually enter a potential target residence. Several of our informants worked sporadically as carpenters' helpers or roofers. During the course of residential construction jobs they became aware of the habits of the people living nearby. They used this knowledge later or provided inside information to other burglars for a fee or a split of the take. Larry, a burglar and heroin addict, told us:

One time I was working on this roofing job in this real nice area. I got to know the schedules of almost everybody on the block. I knew when they left in the morning and came home at night, and who stayed home during the day. About two weeks after the job was done I came back and did [burglarized] almost every house on that block.

BURGLAR ALARMS

A major study of the effectiveness of burglar alarms was conducted by the Cedar Rapids, Iowa, Police Department. Matched pairs of 100 businesses and schools with previous burglaries were chosen for the experiment. One of the pair in each case was given a burglar alarm that sounded directly at the police station. The other half served as a control group. There was a reduction of 55% in attempted burglaries in sites with alarms compared to a reduction of only 8% for the control group (Rubenstein, Murray, Motoyama, & Rouse, 1980). Our findings confirm this prior research. Although several burglars in the present study boasted about disarming alarms, when pressed for details, almost all admitted that they did not know how to accomplish that task. Two informants had disarmed alarm systems and were not particularly deterred by them. They stated that the presence of an alarm system gave them an additional cue as to the affluence of the residents, telling them that there was something worth protecting inside. One informant had purposely taken a job installing alarm systems in order to learn to disarm them. Another informant stated that alarm systems did not deter her because she still had time to complete the burglary and escape before police or private security arrived in response to the alarm. She stated that she never took more than 10 minutes to enter, search, and exit a house. She advised:

Police take 15 to 20 minutes to respond to an alarm. Security [private security] sometimes gets there a little faster. I'm gone before any of them gets there.

Another professional burglar advised that he did not care whether a house had an alarm or not. He would go ahead and enter and begin to gather the goods he planned to steal. He said that after about five minutes the telephone would ring (the alarm company calling to verify the alarm). After the call, he stated that he had 5 to 15 minutes before someone arrived.

In general, however, burglars agreed that alarms were a definite deterrent to their activities. Other factors being equal, they preferred to locate a target that did not have an alarm rather than to take the additional risk involved in attempting to burglarize a house with an alarm system. Over 90% of the informants would not choose a target with an alarm system. Most (about 75%) were deterred by a sign or window sticker that stated that the house was protected by an alarm system. As Richard, an experienced burglar, stated:

Why take a chance? There's lots of places without alarms. Maybe they're bluffing, maybe they ain't.

LOCKS ON DOORS AND WINDOWS

Past research has been inconsistent regarding the importance of locks on windows and doors. Scarr (1973) and Rengert and Wasilchick (1985) found that burglars consider the type of lock installed at a prospective target site. Others (Bennett & Wright, 1984; Reppetto, 1974; Walsh, 1980) did not find locks to be a significant factor in the target selection process.

Research evaluating "target hardening" techniques in four public housing projects in Seattle (1975) and in Chicago's Cabrini-Green public housing (1979) found that installation of deadbolt locks and other such techniques significantly reduced the burglary rate in those areas. From their review of these programs, Rubenstein et al. (1980) concluded that locks are a factor considered by burglars in target selection. The majority of informants in the present study initially stated that they were not deterred by locks, just as in the case of alarm systems. However, during burglary reconstructions, we discovered that given two potential target sites, all other factors being equal, burglars prefer not to deal with a deadbolt lock. Rengert and Wasilchick (1985) wrote: "However, most of the burglars we interviewed are easily discouraged by a tough lock. With so many opportunities, many burglars will move on rather than struggle with a deadbolt lock" (p. 90).

The variation in findings regarding security hardware appears to be related to the degree to which burglars are either rational or opportunistic. To the extent to which burglars are primarily opportunistic, locks appear to have some deterrent value. The opportunistic burglar chooses targets based upon their perceived vulnerability to burglary at a given time. Given a large number of potential targets, the burglar tends to select the most vulnerable of the target pool. A target with a good lock and fitted with other security hardware will usually not be perceived to be as vulnerable as one without those items. The rational, planning burglar chooses targets on the basis of factors other than situational vulnerability and conceives ways in which he or she can overcome impediments to the burglary (such as the target site being fitted with a high quality deadbolt lock). Thus, to the extent that burglars are rational planners, deadbolt locks have limited utility for crime prevention. Our findings support the deterrent value of deadbolt locks; 75% of the burglaries reconstructed during our research were opportunistic offenses. Many of those burglaries would have been prevented (or displaced) by the presence of a quality deadbolt lock. It is important to note that nearly one half of the burglary sites in the present study were entered through open or unlocked windows and doors. The findings are very similar to those of Rengert & Wasilchick (1985) who found that burglary through unlocked doors was a "surprisingly frequent occurrence." They wrote:

> Many burglars build their careers on the mistaken belief held by residents that "it can't happen here," or "I'll only be next door for a minute." More than one of the burglars we talked to burglarized open houses while the residents were in the backyard doing yard work. (p. 90)

DOGS

Almost all studies agree that dogs are an effective deterrent to burglary. Although there is some individual variation among burglars, the general rule is to bypass a house with a dog—any dog. Large dogs represent a physical threat to the burglar and small ones are often noisy, attracting attention to the burglar's activities. We found that although many burglars have developed contingency plans to deal with dogs (petting them, feeding them, or even killing them), most burglars prefer to avoid them. When asked what were considered absolute "no go" factors, most burglars responded that dogs were second only to occupancy.

Approximately 30% of the informants, however, initially discounted the presence of dogs as a deterrent. Yet, during ride alongs the sight or sound of a dog at a potential target site almost invariably resulted in a "no go" decision. As Richard said:

I don't mess with no dogs. If they got dogs I go someplace else.

Debbie told us that she was concerned primarily with small dogs:

Big dogs don't bark much. I talk to them through the fence or door and get them excited. Then I open the gate or the door and when they charge out, I go in and shut the door behind me. They are outside and I'm in. Little dogs yap too much. They [neighbors] look to see what they are so excited about. I don't like little yapping dogs.

Some of the more professional burglars were less concerned with dogs and had developed techniques for dealing with them. In general, however, the presence of a dog was considered an effective deterrent.

3

The Decision Strategy

Our findings suggest that a burglar's decision to hit a target is based primarily on environmental cues that are perceived to have immediate consequences. Most burglars appear to attend only to the present; future events or consequences do not appear to weigh heavily in their risk-versus-gain calculation. Drug-using burglars and juveniles are particularly oriented to this immediate-gain and immediate-risk decision process. Non-drug-using experienced burglars are probably less likely to attend only to immediate risks and gains. Our informants, although experienced burglars, were all drug users, and tended to have a "here and now" orientation toward the rewards and costs associated with burglary.

The decision strategy employed by our informants began with an initial heuristic to weigh gain versus risk by asking the general question: Do the immediate gains outweigh the immediate risks? We found that burglars tend to assume that all potential target sites contain something worth stealing. Most burglars in the study expended minimal energy and time assessing gain cues. They estimated potential gain quickly and intuitively. They have established a minimal expectation of gain; that is, they expect to net some minimal dollar amount from each burglary. Their basic assumption was that all residences contained at least something worth stealing. Debbie, a professional burglar, illustrated this assumption while assessing one neighborhood:

Every house has got something worth stealing. I figure to get $50 every time I go in a place.

They also tend to make assessments of individual target sites based upon their evaluation of the general affluence of the neighborhood in which the target is located. The assumption is that most residences in a neighborhood contain essentially the same quality and quantity of "stealable" items. Luis, a heroin addict/burglar, told the interviewer:

Most houses in this neighborhood have got at least two color TVs, a VCR, some stereo equipment, and some good jewelry. A lot of 'em have got guns, too.

Beyond assuming a minimal level of expected gain from each site and a standard level of gain from each site in a particular neighborhood, burglars also conduct a cursory assessment of gain cues at each specific target site. James, a very experienced burglar, asserted:

I look for those satellite TV dishes. If they got one of those they got expensive electronic stuff inside.

Mario, another experienced burglar, said:

If you see a Jeep in the driveway or a RV [recreational vehicle] or a boat, you can usually find some sporting equipment. A lot of the time you find guns.

Jesse preferred to assess a particular site by the type of automobile usually parked there. He said:

If they got an old wreck parked outside, they don't have nothing. It's not worth the time. I look for a new car. Something like an Oldsmobile.

As burglars gain experience or when their drug habits require more money, their minimal expectation from each burglary increases and they may move their search area to higher income neighborhoods. With the move to another neighborhood, the expected gain increases. A burglar who was once satisfied with $50 per burglary may now expect $100 from each target site. In a sense, however, the expected gain is a constant, for the burglar manipulates the expected gain by changing the search area to one with greater potential. By assuming a minimal gain potential at each site, the burglar may concentrate on assessing risk cues during the decision process.

ASSESSING RISK

Immediate risks, unlike immediate gains, are not assumed to be constant, and vary widely from target site to target site. The net effect is that when only the immediate gains and risks are weighed, and some minimal gain is assumed, the burglar has only to assess risks and then rule out sites that are perceived to pose risks that exceed those which he or she is willing to assume given the expected gain.

The immediate risk cues considered by burglars in the target selection decision are of three types: "surveillability", occupancy, and accessibility.

Surveillability refers to the extent to which a house is overseen and observable by neighbors or passersby. Surveillability cues include the location of the house on the block, visibility of the target site from neighbors' houses, and visibility from the street of doors and other entry points. The surveillability of a potential burglary target was considered by our informants as a primary factor in target selection. These cues provide answers to several questions of primary importance to the burglar. Are there neighbors present? Can the neighbors observe the target house from inside their homes? Can the proposed point of entry into the target site be observed by passersby? Are there dogs that might bark and arouse neighbors? Are there shrubs, blind doorways, corners, or fences that will hide the burglar during entry? Is there traffic near the house that might see and report the burglar? Are there people in the neighborhood who "watch the street and know who is and who is not at home"?

The location and type of windows both at the target site and at neighbors' houses were considered critical by almost all informants. One informant stated:

Notice how that picture window looks out onto the street. The curtains stay open all the time and both the houses across the street can see straight into the living room. I wouldn't do [burglarize] this place.

Another said:

I'm looking at that upstairs window next door. You can see almost everything that goes on at this house from there. I'm worried about that window.

Although the average burglar fears being seen, many professional burglars do not. Rather, they fear being seen *and reported*. The more experienced burglars stated that it was important to fit into a neighborhood or situation. They attempted to make their presence in a neighborhood seem normal and natural. The most professional of the burglars in our study, Robert, always drove a car that fit the neighborhood's socioeconomic level or a van disguised as a delivery vehicle. He dressed befitting the circumstances: as a plumber, deliveryman, or businessman. He would walk to the door of a potential target residence, open the screen door, and unobtrusively hold it open with his foot while he pantomimed a conversation with a nonexistent person inside. He would then enter the house if the door was unlocked (he reported that many of his target houses were unlocked). If the door was locked, he pantomimed a conversation that appeared to instruct him to go around to the backyard. He would then walk around the house, sometimes stopping to gaze at some feature of the house or landscape, and take notes on a clipboard. When he got to the backyard, he entered the house from that point. To possible onlookers, he had knocked on the door, talked with the owner, and, following instructions, had gone to the rear of the house on some legitimate errand.

Other times he would stop his car near a proposed target residence, open the hood, tinker around under the hood, appear to be angry, kick a tire, and angrily walk over to the potential target house. A neighbor or anyone else who might be watching saw only an angry man with a broken car, walking to a house to ask for assistance.

Robert was not concerned about being seen. He expected to be seen, but because of his role-playing he did not expect to be reported (and he seldom was).

Surveillability cues also include the extent of natural cover such as trees, shrubbery, and other landscaping. Houses with dense shrubbery near windows and doors were considered very vulnerable by the informants. One of the most important forms of cover was the privacy fence, a six- to eight-foot-high board or masonry fence enclosing a backyard. These fences were common in the area studied, and most informants considered them important in the target selection process. Some stated that they would not consider burglarizing a house that did not have a privacy fence. Although burglars were at risk while climbing the fence or entering through an unlocked gate, once inside, they were effectively protected from prying eyes by the fence. As one burglar stated:

Once I'm inside this fence, I can slow down and take my time. The place is mine.

The second category of risk cues are those that indicate *occupancy*. Occupancy cues are considered immediately after the burglar determines that he or she is not likely to be observed and reported while in the act of committing the burglary. Occupancy cues include the presence of cars in the driveway or garage, visible residents, noise or voices emanating from the house, and other cues that indicate someone is at home.

Prior research has consistently reported that a primary concern of the residential burglar is whether or not a target site is occupied. Twenty-eight of the 30 burglars in our study stated that they would never purposely enter an occupied residence. Many reported that their greatest fear was that they would encounter the resident upon entering or that the resident would return home while they were still there. The burglar, therefore, not only scans the physical environment for signs of occupancy, he or she also probes the proposed target site to determine if it is occupied (see the discussion of occupancy probes in Chapter 2).

Accessibility cues are those factors that indicate how easily the residence can be entered and how well the site is protected. These cues include location and type of doors and windows, as well as the extent of target hardening such as locks, burglar alarms, fences, walls, burglar bars, and dogs.

USING RISK CUES

We found that most burglars use a simple yet highly efficient three-component decision-making strategy (see also Walsh, 1980). The decision model rests on two assumptions. The first assumption is that burglars are not attempting to maximize outcomes. They are generally seeking satisfactory target choices rather than optimal ones. The decision model can best be described a *satisficing* strategy rather than an optimizing one.[7] The second assumption is that burglars expect some minimal gain from each potential burglary target. Holding gain as a constant, risk cues then are assessed to answer the question: Do the immediate risks exceed the minimal expectation of gain?

Burglars appear to utilize a decision-making procedure termed *argument by contradiction*. For each component of the decision process the burglar makes an assumption about the true condition and then searches the environment for risk cues to contradict it. The first component of the decision process is directed at determining surveillability. The operating assumption is: "Someone will see and report me." The second component addresses occupancy. The operating assumption is: "Someone is home." The third component concerns accessibility. The essential features of accessibility concern the ease of access and exit. The operating assumption is: "Entry is too difficult." Figure 3.1 illustrates this decision-making process.

The burglar makes an initial assumption (Someone will observe and report my activity), assumes that it is true, and then searches the immediate physical environment for evidence that contradicts it. If a contradiction is found (The neighborhood appears deserted), the initial assumption is rejected. When only two conclusions can logically be reached, the alternative conclusion is accepted by default (No one will observe or report my activity).

For example, if the initial assumption is "Someone is at home," and the burglar observes several days' accumulation of mail in the mailbox, three daily newspapers on the lawn, and no one answers the doorbell, then such evidence can be taken to contradict the initial assumption. He or she may now logically conclude, "No one is home."

The components of the decision process appear to be addressed sequentially. Most burglars in our study assessed cues relating to surveillability first, cues relating to occupancy second, and cues relating to accessibility last. Clearly, however, the order in which burglars address each component may vary among burglars. The order may even vary from context to context. Furthermore, the assumptions of occupancy, surveillability, and accessibility may be assessed simultaneously. The critical point is that all three components must be addressed before a decision to burglarize is made. Such a three-component decision process maximizes the burglar's outcomes by minimizing the risks. However, the decision *not* to enter is made whenever information consistent with *any* operating assumption is found. Thus such a decision-making strategy is biased toward personal safety because the decision to proceed is always reached through a more complex and time-consuming process than the decision to abort.

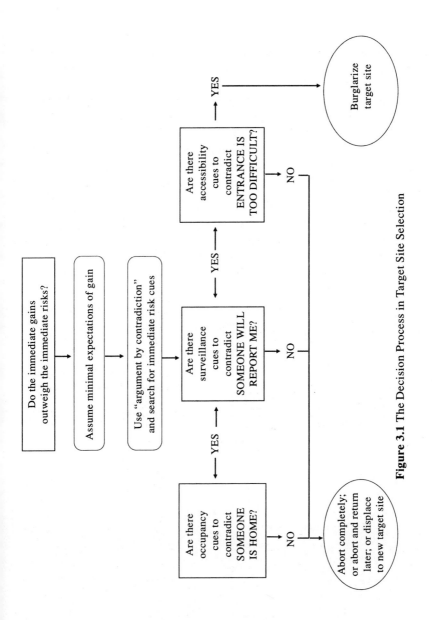

Figure 3.1 The Decision Process in Target Site Selection

SUMMARY

Burglars employ a decision-making strategy that has three components. The burglar begins with an assumption that each proposed target site contains at least some minimal potential gain. He or she must then determine whether the target site can be entered without being seen and reported, whether the site might be occupied, and whether the site can be broken into readily. These determinations are made on the basis of evidence obtained from observing environmental cues at or near the target site.

We found burglars use three categories of environmental cues to assess these risk factors: (a) cues that indicate the surveillability of the proposed target site, (b) cues that indicate whether the target site is occupied, and (c) cues that indicate the degree of difficulty that might be expected in actually breaking into the site. The specific content of these cues has varied widely across prior studies.

We found that burglars are opportunistic and are easily deterred or displaced from one target site to another. Situational factors such as the presence of a dog, an alarm system, security hardware, and alert neighbors may be the most effective deterrents.

When one or more of these risk cues are discerned by the burglar, the target is usually considered too risky and the burglary is aborted. This is especially true for the opportunistic burglar and less so for the non-drug-using professional. These findings have particular relevance for crime prevention, because they suggest that burglary is more easily prevented by situational measures than previously thought.

4

The Rational and the Opportunistic Burglar

There were substantial differences between our findings and those of previous research efforts in several critical areas. Unlike in previous research, our informants were "free world" active burglars. We interviewed them in their own social and physical environment and we went with them to reconstruct their past crimes. We found important variations between what they initially told us (in the relatively structured interview setting of Session 1) about the process of selecting a target and committing a burglary, and what they actually did when presented with a field simulation. For instance, during Session 1 many informants specified the attributes of a desirable burglary target and discussed the manner in which they would case, probe, and ultimately commit a hypothetical burglary. However, when subsequently visiting sites of burglaries they had previously committed, the characteristics of the target sites and the techniques used to burglarize those targets were seldom congruent with the completely rational approach they had reconstructed during the earlier interview. The sites, more often than not, were targets of opportunity rather than purposeful selections. There were three common patterns: (a) The burglar happened by the potential burglary site at an opportune moment when the occupants were clearly absent and the target was perceived as vulnerable (open garage door, windows, etc.); (b) the site was one that had been previously visited by the burglar for a legitimate purpose (as a guest, delivery person, maintenance worker, or other such activity); (c) the site was chosen after "cruising" neighborhoods searching for a criminal opportunity and detecting some overt or subtle cue as to vulnerability or potential for material gain.

RATIONAL RECONSTRUCTION

Most of our burglar informants could design a textbook burglary. During Session 1 they often described their past burglaries as though they were rationally conceived and executed. Yet upon closer inspection, when their previous burglaries were reconstructed, textbook procedures frequently gave way to opportunity and situational factors. This phenomenon might be termed *rational reconstruction.*

We suggest that research reporting that a high percentage of burglars make carefully planned, highly rational decisions based upon a detailed evaluation of environmental cues may be in error. Our findings indicate that burglars interviewed in prison or those recalling crimes from the past, either consciously or unconsciously, may engage in rational re-construction—a reinterpretation of past behavior through which the actor recasts activities in a manner consistent with "what should have been" rather than "what was." This phenomenon is no different than what might be observed after asking a police officer how he or she conducts an interrogation. Most will respond in a manner consistent with departmental policy and procedures. However, in a real-life situation, the officer may have developed procedures of his or her own and may utilize techniques gained on the streets or learned from fellow officers rather than those learned in the police academy. If a researcher wishes to know how police officers conduct interrogations, real-life observations will provide more valid data than interviews. The same is true for understanding burglars and how they function.

We found substantial differences between the information obtained during the office interview during Session 1 and what the informants actually did before, during, and after their real burglaries. Few burglars would initially admit to being opportunistic. Professionalism, creativity, and inventiveness are valued attributes among burglars, and simple opportunism is not consistent with the self-image of most burglars. Past criminal events tend to be remembered as though committed in a manner consistent with their self-image.

This is not a matter of lack of knowledge about the techniques of burglary or the ability to discriminate between vulnerable and risky targets. Most burglars, even novices, appear to know how to discriminate a vulnerable residence from one that is less vulnerable. As seen in Table 4.1, the informants successfully discriminated target sites that had been previously burglarized by other burglars from those that were designated as high risks by other burglars.

Table 4.1 High Risk Versus Previously Hit Burglary Ratings

| | | Hypothetical Circumstances | |
Site	At present (now)	Assuming no one is home	Assuming no one is home and $250 cash is inside
High risk	2.12 (135)	4.31 (117)	5.36 (109)
Previously hit	3.72 (136)	5.93 (114)	7.01 (106)
	$F(1,249) = 17.09$ $p < .05$	$F(1,213) = 10.41$ $p < .05$	$F(1,199) = 12.08$ $p < .05$

The individual burglary attractiveness ratings (means) of burglars alone under the circumstances that actually prevailed at the time of the site inspection (now) and hypothetical circumstances for high risk and previously hit sites. The number of individual ratings from which each mean was obtained is given in parentheses. The results of two-sample tests comparing high risk and previously hit means are given below.

Control subjects ($n = 20$) also rated the previously burglarized and high risk sites. Table 4.2 reveals that they, too, could discriminate between more vulnerable and less vulnerable targets. They did, however, generally rate the sites higher (more vulnerable) than did the actual burglars. This is most likely attributable to the burglars' experience in discriminating risk cues relating to occupancy; in the hypothetical situations (assuming no one is at home) the ratings of control subjects generally did not consistently discriminate high risk from previously hit targets.

Although data from the control subjects indicate that novices can discriminate between vulnerable and less vulnerable targets about as well as burglars, it is doubtful that they know how a "proper" burglary should be conducted. On the other hand, our informants, including the least experienced, were capable of describing how a rationally conceived burglary would be planned and conducted. This is probably the result of information shared on the streets and in jails and reformatories.

ROUTINE ACTIVITIES

Our study concludes that a completely rational model of decision making in residential burglary cannot be supported. Rather, the study

Table 4.2 High Risk Versus Previously Hit Burglary Ratings for Controls

		Hypothetical Circumstances	
Site	At present (now)	Assuming no one is home	Assuming no one is home and $250 cash is inside
High risk	3.20 (359)	5.13 (358)	6.12 (359)
Previously hit	4.77 (251)	5.78 (270)	6.38 (263)
	$t(608) = 7.05$ $p < .05$	$t(626) = 2.80$ $p < .05$	$t(620) = 0.87$ $p > .05$

The individual burglary attractiveness ratings (means) of control subjects under the circumstances that actually prevailed at the time of the site inspection (now) and hypothetical circumstances for high risk and previously hit sites. The number of individual ratings from which mean was obtained is given in parentheses. The results of two-sample tests comparing high risk and previously hit means are given below.

tends to support a *limited rationality* model; specifically Cohen and Felson's (1979) concept of "routine activities." *Routine activities* is an opportunity theory that holds that normal movement and activities of both potential victims and potential offenders play a role in the occurrence of the criminal event. Cohen and Felson link criminal events to the interaction of three variables:

(1) the presence of motivated offenders,
(2) the availability of suitable targets, and
(3) the absence of capable guardians.

When these variables converge, there is a greater likelihood that a crime will occur.

Routine activities theory has been used to explain the rise in crime rates over the past 30 years. The authors conclude that the number of caretakers (guardians) at home during the day has decreased because more women are participating in the work force, leaving a greater percentage of homes unguarded during the day. With the decline of the traditional neighborhood, other guardians (friends, neighbors) have dwindled. Furthermore, the supply of marketable, easily transportable goods (jewelry, TVs, VCRs) has increased, making the volume of available targets much greater. With the coming of age of the baby boomers between 1960 and 1980, there was an increase of the number of motivated offenders and thus an increase in the predatory crime rate (Siegel, 1989).

Routine activities theory focuses on the life-styles of both offenders and victims. Cohen and Felson (1979) found that time spent away from home was significantly related to the level of crime. Activities away from home increase the level of interaction between victim and criminal and thereby the probability that a criminal event will occur (Lab, 1988). Time spent in activities away from home also leaves the home unguarded, increasing the probability that the home will be burglarized.

The normal activities of criminals also affect crime rates. Offenders are more likely to commit crimes if their daily activities bring them into contact with potential victims. When questioned as to how a particular residence was selected as a burglary target, the responses given by informants were frequently consistent with routine activities theory.

Jesse, a professional burglar, stated:

When I was younger I used to ride my bicycle over to the skating rink. If I saw a house that I liked while I was coming to the rink, I'd do it [burglarize] on the way home.

Ramon, Jesse's co-offender, explained his approach to target selection:

When I'm going to work or over to a friend's house or someplace, I keep my eyes out for a good place to hit. I've been watching this one house on my way to work for a couple of weeks.

Debbie explained her reason for choosing a particular neighborhood to commit a large number of burglaries:

These people out here [lower middle-class neighborhood] don't have much money. You know the wives got to work and there aren't hardly any of them home during the day. I come out here about 9:00 [a.m.] and have the whole neighborhood to myself.

Stefan, an experienced burglar, described another neighborhood:

This neighborhood is full of families with kids in elementary school. I don't do this part of town in the summer. Too many kids playing around. But now [February] the best time to do crime out here is between 8:00 and 9:00 [a.m.].

All the mothers are taking the kids to school. I wait until I see the car leave. By the time she gets back, I've come and gone.

Quantitative Support for Routine Activities Theory

To partially validate the ethnographic data supporting routine activities, we compared 300 previously burglarized residences to 300 residences with no official record of having been burglarized. Each residence was evaluated in terms of its attributes on variables relevant to routine activities theory: distance from the residence to the nearest corner, and distance from the residence to the nearest stop sign, traffic light, school, commercial business establishment, park, church, and four-lane street. Other variables included the number of lanes of traffic in front of the residence, the average speed of traffic in front of the residence, and the presence or absence of a garage or carport.

Table 4.3 displays the results of the stepwise discriminant analysis performed to determine which variables best discriminated between the burglarized and nonburglarized sites. The resulting discriminant function accounted for over 50% of the variability between burglarized and nonburglarized residences and correctly classified 90.5% of the burglarized residences and 80% of the nonburglarized targets. Separate Pearson correlations indicated that the slower the traffic in front of the residence and the closer the residence was located to a school, church, corner, stop sign/light, or four lane street (other than a four lane business street), the greater the likelihood the residence would be burglarized. The presence or absence of a garage was also a discriminating variable. Residences with no garage or those with open carports were more likely to be burglarized than those with a garage. Our informants explained that it was easier to discern whether someone was at home when they could easily observe if there was a car parked at the site, indicating that the resident was home.

These results tend to suggest that as burglars go about their everyday activities, traveling to and from activity hubs such as school, work, and recreational facilities, they come into contact with residential sites near those facilities. Residences on or near their transportation routes (four lane streets) are also potential burglary targets. When burglars stop at a traffic light or stop sign they have a brief opportunity to view the sites nearby and may choose a potential target during those moments. It is possible that this (rather than the surveillance explanation) accounts for the disproportionate selection of corner houses as burglary targets.

Table 4.3 Burglarized Versus Nonburglarized Residences

Stepwise discriminant analysis among physical attributes related to whether a residence was burglarized. The .05 criterion level was used for inclusion in the analysis.

Attributes	Correlation within the stepwise discriminant function	Separate Pearson correlations with burglarization	Significance of separate Pearson correlations
Distance to school[a]	.66	.57	$p < .05$
Driving speed[a]	.47	.27	$p < .05$
Distance to four lane[a]	.41	.41	$p < .05$
Garage absent[a]	.33	.37	$p < .05$
Distance to business[a]	−.18	−.03	$p > .05$
Assessed value	—	.25	$p < .05$
Carport absent	—	.18	$p < .05$
Distance to corner	—	.14	$p < .05$
Distance to stop sign	—	.14	$p < .05$
Distance to church	—	.08	$p < .05$
Distance to park	—	.01	$p > .05$
Number of street lanes in front	—	−.13	$p < .05$

a. These five variables entered the discriminant function that accounted for over 50% of the variation between burglarized and nonburglarized sites with a Wilks' lambda of .49 (X^2 (5) = 429.83, $p < .01$) and correctly classified 90.5% of the burglarized sites and 80% of the nonburglarized sites.

Thirty-nine percent of the burglarized houses were located on a corner. Approximately 25% of the houses studied were corner houses.

OPPORTUNITY AND BURGLARY

Although the professional burglars among our informants tended to select targets in a purposive manner, analyzing the physical and social characteristics of the environment and choosing targets congruent with the template developed from experience, by far the greater proportion of the informants were opportunistic. The targets they chose appeared particularly vulnerable—at the time. Thus most burglaries in the jurisdiction studied appeared to result from the propitious juxtaposition of target, offender, and situation.

An opportunistic burglar is not necessarily an amateur. Selecting targets by completely rational processes does not alone differentiate the

skilled (professional or journeyman burglar) from the novice or amateur. As stated earlier, opportunism does not necessarily imply lack of
rationality. A burglar may make a completely rational decision to take
advantage of certain criminal opportunities when they arise or to seek
out or even create opportunities in a systematic manner.

TYPOLOGIES OF BURGLARS

Bennett and Wright (1984) found three categories of burglars: planners, searchers, and opportunists. The *planner* selects a target well in
advance of the offense; the *searcher* reconnoiters an area seeking out a
suitable target; and the *opportunist* responds "there and then" to an
attractive set of environmental cues—for example, an open garage door
at a site that is apparently unoccupied at the precise time the potential
burglar arrives on the scene. Bennett and Wright concluded that only
7% of their sample of 117 burglars were opportunists. They found it
"surprising that so few offenders mentioned committing opportunistic
crimes" (p. 44), and suggested that their limited definition of "opportunistic" and the age and experience level of their sample might account
for the small number of opportunistic burglars.[8]
We chose a broader definition of *opportunist,* one that incorporated
two of Bennett and Wright's categories: searcher and opportunist. The
searcher takes advantage of sought out opportunities and the opportunist responds to presented opportunities. We considered burglars in both
categories to be opportunists. The opportunist may commit the burglary
immediately after searching the target or may wait until the situation is
more advantageous for the commission of a criminal act. Bennett and
Wright (1984) delineated between the searcher and opportunist categories on the basis of the elapsed time between perception of the criminal
opportunity and commission of the crime. The searcher allowed time to
pass between locating a target and committing the burglary (presumably
for planning purposes); the opportunist committed the burglary there
and then. With the exception of very inexperienced juveniles, few
burglars (and none in our sample) fit the Bennett and Wright (1984)
definition of opportunistic. Whether or not a burglar waits and plans
after site selection appears to be determined more by the immediate
situation than by his or her orientation as opportunistic or planner (or
irrational versus rational).

Opportunism, by our definition, turns on the target selection process, not on the time between selection and commission of the burglary. A rational process might well necessitate taking advantage there and then of a particular juxtaposition of situational factors. For example, while reconstructing a past burglary, Ramon stated:

I saw this place one day when I was cruising looking for a place to hit. It looked perfect, but it was too big to do alone. I needed a posse [gang of burglars]. I got me three other dudes and went back about a week later and did it.

He explained that the house appealed to him because of the apparent affluence of the residents, the secluded location of the house on the lot, and an unlocked garage door. However, the house was very large and could be approached from several directions. He feared that without lookouts and extra persons to search once inside, the risk would be too great. His decision to burglarize the site was an opportunistic one, although his process was that of a planner. Several other prior burglaries reconstructed by the same individual were purely opportunistic. In one instance, he "happened by" a vulnerable target while on his way home from a party. The site was vulnerable right then. He committed the burglary with no further planning than to probe briefly to determine whether the house was occupied. Although unquestionably opportunistic, the burglary was nonetheless rational: The site was unoccupied, a window was open, and the neighborhood appeared to be deserted. He could not have expected to find a more advantageous set of circumstances than those that were presented there and then.

Exploiting opportunity characterized the target selection processes in over 75% of the burglaries reconstructed during our research. Even professional burglars among our informants often took advantage of presented opportunities when they arose. Chance opportunities occasionally presented themselves while the professional was casing and probing potential burglary targets chosen by more rational means. When these opportunities arose, the professional burglar was as likely as other burglars to take advantage of the situation.

Our subjects can be placed along a continuum, with the novice burglar at one pole, the professional at the other, and the journeyman near the center.

The novice is at the beginning of his or her career as a burglar or a juvenile who commits one or more burglaries and then desists. The novice frequently learns from older, more experienced burglars in the same neighborhood. These older burglars are often relatives, frequently older siblings. The novice is usually initially allowed to go along with the older burglars, acting as the "lookout" for the older youth. As the novice learns the techniques of burglary, he or she may become a permanent member of the older group of burglars or may take the knowledge gained from the older group back to his or her own peer group and begin committing burglaries with the younger group without continued supervision from the older burglars.

A major determinant of whether the novice stays with the older group or returns to his or her own age cohort is whether he or she can locate and develop a market for the property obtained from burglaries (see Chapter 5, "Developmental Processes of Drug Use and Burglary" for a more detailed discussion). Older mentors, who teach novices the techniques of burglary, often conceal the identity of their fences. Until younger burglars can find a regular market for their stolen property, they have to depend on the older burglar. Even when they go out on their own they must rely on their mentors to sell the property for them (and pay a fee or a percentage of the gains). Once the market is established, however, the novice may advance along the continuum toward the journeyman level. Four of the informants in the present study were novice burglars.

Once an individual has mastered the technical and organizational skills, made the requisite contacts for marketing stolen property, and developed what Sutherland (1937) called a "larceny sense," he or she may be considered a *journeyman* burglar. The journeyman category corresponds roughly to Shover's (1971) "serious thief." Journeymen are experienced, reliable burglars. The burglary style of the journeyman burglar is marked by a preference for searching out or creating opportunities, much like the searcher category identified by Bennett and Wright (1984) and the suburban burglar studied by Rengert and Wasilchick (1985). Rather than waiting for criminal opportunities to present themselves during ordinary daily activities, the journeyman searches out or creates opportunities. Selecting a community or neighborhood in which he or she feels comfortable, the burglar cruises around looking for a target site that looks vulnerable. The burglar may plan the act by casing the site for a period of a few hours to several days to assess the ease or difficulty of access and egress. Assistance in the form of additional persons may be necessary and the burglar may require time to put a team together. He or she may also determine that the situation and circumstances make a there-and-then hit advantageous and commit the crime immediately after target selection. In our study, 21 of the informants were classified as journeymen.

Professional burglars constitute the elite of the burglary world. They are differentiated from the other categories by the level of their technical skill, their organizational abilities, and the status accorded them by peers and generally by law enforcement authorities. Professionals do no usually commit crimes of opportunity. They plan and execute their crimes with deliberation. They have excellent contacts for disposing of stolen merchandise. They may or may not be drug addicts. Drug addiction does not preclude the designation *professional*. The primary difference between the professional and the journeyman burglar is the status accorded to each. Their status is recognized and accepted by others (other thieves, law enforcement, fences, etc.), and they are accorded "respect" befitting that status. Five of the informants in our study were considered professional burglars.

SUMMARY

We found considerable disparity between what burglars divulged in interviews during Sessions 1 and 2, and what they actually did while committing their crimes. We suggest that prior research, which involved interviewing burglars in prisons, jails, or in probation and parole settings, may have arrived at erroneous conclusions based upon misleading information supplied by the informants. We use the term *rational reconstruction* to describe the tendency of burglars (and other persons) to describe past events as though they were performed in the ideal or proper fashion. Our research technique, staged activity analysis, was devised to overcome this problem. The data we obtained through the use of this design should be more reliable and valid than data obtained from interviews alone. We concluded that burglars are less rational (and more opportunistic) than indicated by most previous research.

5

Drug and Group Effects on Burglars' Decision Making

Research has consistently shown that a large proportion of property offenders are addicted to drugs or have used illegal drugs in the recent past (Bureau of Justice Statistics [BJS], 1988; Johnson et al., 1985; National Institute of Justice [NIJ], 1989b). If drug usage (and concomitant arousal and disequilibrium) affects the rational, sequential decision model of target selection by residential burglars, and if a substantial proportion of burglars are drug abusers, decision-making models that assume a rational cognitive state are limited in what they can explain, how well they predict behavior, and how generally they apply. One of the purposes of the present study is to determine how drug use affects burglary target selection and other decision-making processes of residential burglars, with particular emphasis on the influence of drugs on the rational decision model.

We also wished to discern the influence of the presence of co-offenders on the decision-making process. Some previous literature suggests that group decisions differ from individual decisions in very significant ways (Shaw, 1981; Zajonc, 1965, 1980). Do group decisions tend to be riskier decisions, as some have suggested, or might they become more cautious? Are burglars who work with partners apprehended more often than those who work alone? Do burglars who work with partners have a higher rate of offending? Do drug effects interact with group effects? How do these issues influence the rational decision-making model?

PREVALENCE OF DRUG USING BURGLARS

Our findings suggest that the percentage of drug using burglars is much greater than that reported in prior studies. During Session 1 about one half of the informants admitted to regular illicit drug use. As we developed rapport and trust with the informants, however, or when we confronted an informant whom we believed to be misrepresenting his or her drug use, we found that all of the informants were either drug addicts or regular users of illegal drugs. Because previous research (Åkerström, 1983; Bennett & Wright, 1984; Reppetto, 1974) has reported a much smaller percentage (30% to 60%) of drug users in burglar populations, we were concerned initially that our sample was biased in favor of drug users. Consequently, we attempted to actively recruit non-drug-using burglars. Both our informants and local law enforcement officials, however, advised us that there were virtually no burglars in the area who were not drug users. Although this finding could be an artifact of the sampling procedure or of the geographic locale where the study was conducted, it suggests that prior research using incarcerated burglars as informants may have underestimated the prevalence of drug use among burglars. Previous studies have relied on incarcerated burglars or burglars on probation or parole as informants. The interviews were usually not conducted over a long period of time and the researchers did not have the opportunity to interact with the informants for a period of time sufficient to develop rapport and trust. There is little reason to believe that informants are completely truthful with researchers during one or two interviews conducted in circumstances that might appear threatening (in prison, probation offices, etc.). Our informants were contacted outside criminal justice channels, yet one half of them initially denied drug use. Their subsequent admission to drug use came only after the third or fourth interview, and then sometimes only after being confronted about inconsistencies in their story.[9]

Although the high incidence of drug use among our informants is not consistent with previous research, it is more consistent with recent Drug Use Forecasting System (NIJ, 1989a, 1989b) data, which revealed that between 54% and 90% of male arrestees tested during a two-month period in 21 cities showed evidence of recent drug use. The report found that in most cities two to four times more drug users were detected by urinalysis than by self-reports. The NIJ data also suggest that the percentage of drug using criminals is steadily increasing.

INTERDEPENDENCE OF DRUGS AND BURGLARY

Our findings reveal an interdependence between drug abuse and residential burglary. This does not, however, imply that drug use is implicated in the etiology of burglary. In fact, most of our informants committed their first burglary before they began regular drug use (see also Faupel, 1987; Faupel & Klockars, 1987). Once they began to use drugs regularly, however, they usually began to rely, at least partially, on criminal activity to maintain the habit. As their drug use intensified, the users (particularly heroin addicts) found regular employment increasingly difficult to maintain, and they often dropped out of legitimate society and into a drug-using, criminal subculture. Thereafter, most maintained their drug habit through full-time criminal activity. Because drug users must establish and maintain illicit contacts in order to buy drugs, they are drawn further into a network of criminal associates, and thus more deeply into a deviant life-style.

Developmental Processes of Drug Use and Burglary

The typical pattern of entry into the life-style of burglary and drug abuse among our informants was as follows:

(1) At about age 10 to 13, adolescents in a generally criminogenic environment were allowed to join a group of older (14 to 17) adolescents who either shoplifted or committed a burglary. This crime was usually committed in the neighborhood in which they all lived. The younger members were allowed to share in the proceeds, although they almost never received an equal share. If the property stolen was cash or later converted to cash, they bought candy, cigarettes, video game tokens, and so forth with their share. More frequently the younger members of the group were allowed to keep small items such as radios, jam boxes, or toys. They used these items or traded them for other items.

(2) This activity typically occurred 3 to 10 times before the younger apprentices either progressed to doing a burglary more or less on their own or they became accepted as a more integral part of the older group. If they formed their own gang, the first burglary on their own (usually in groups of two or three) frequently resulted in a small amount of stolen property that they could not easily convert to cash because of lack of contacts to fence the goods. They kept the items or agreed to share their proceeds with an older, more experienced burglar in exchange for marketing the stolen property.

(3) At this point, typically from one to six months after the first burglary with the older adolescents, they often began to buy alcohol, pills, or marijuana with some of the proceeds, or to trade the stolen property for drugs and alcohol.

(4) As they grew more confident and gained more experience (and criminal associates), they located an outlet—a local fence or a middleman to act as a go-between in disposing of the stolen property. In this manner they found themselves on the fringe of a delinquent/drug-using subculture. Drugs were now readily available and the youths now had money to purchase them.

(5) The adolescents found that drugs and burglary facilitated each other. Smoking marijuana, crack cocaine, or drinking alcohol made the burglaries easier by reducing fear and inhibitions. Thereafter, burglaries were frequently committed under the influence of drugs and the proceeds were used to buy (or barter for) more drugs.

(6) The focus of activity among the adolescents then changed from a focal concern with the excitement and thrills (Miller, 1958) and peer approval that came with committing burglaries to the use and abuse of drugs and alcohol. Burglary and other property crime became only a means of achieving the wherewithal to buy drugs. In a sense, the two activities could no longer be separated. They were two sides of the same coin, having evolved together in the adolescents' immediate past history.

When questioned as to whether they would be committing burglaries if they were not using drugs, virtually all of the informants stated they would not, or that their rate of offending would be much lower. Reppetto (1974) concluded that if drug abuse were cured or if drug addicts had their habits met in some way that did not require them to steal, "a major drop in Boston residential burglary rates would ensue" (p. 72). We agree that some types of criminal activity might be reduced; however, most of our informants also cited the excitement of the crime itself, the need for money to maintain a "fast life," and the independence of a life of crime as additional motivations for their burglaries.

THE RATIONAL ADDICT

Preble and Casey (1969) were the first to challenge the traditional image of the addict-criminal as an irrational "dope fiend." Their study of heroin addicts in New York City presented a view of the addict as a hard-driving career person whom they compared to a business executive. Our findings, as well as other recent research, support this characterization of the heroin addict (Faupel, 1987; Faupel & Klockars, 1987; Inciardi, 1979; Johnson et al., 1985). We believe that the addict might best be viewed as an entrepreneur who must be skilled and dedicated in order to survive. Unlike stereotypical dope fiends, the heroin addicts we interviewed approached burglary as an occupation, invariably referring to their crimes as work (see also Letkemann, 1973). Rico, a heroin addict, said:

I think of this as work just like you think of your job as work. You are a professor, I'm a junkie and a burglar.

Debbie, a female heroin addict, stated:

I get up every morning and go to "work." Before I comb my hair or brush my teeth, I go out and steal something to get $20 for a "fix." After I've fixed for the first time, I clean up and go to work again.

She explained that when she had failed to hold back some heroin from the night before, her first crime of the day was often unplanned and sometimes even desperate. "I steal anything," she said, "tools from the back of a truck or I break into a car and take something. It doesn't make much difference what it is or how dangerous it is. I need that first fix real bad." After her first fix, however, her crimes, usually burglaries, had a certain elegance in their planning and execution. She was proud of her work and the fact that, although she had been stealing daily for eight years, she had been arrested only twice and convicted only once. She received probation for that conviction because she was a first offender.

Controlling the Habit

The ability of heroin addicts to manage and regulate their addiction has been reported in several recent studies. Bruce Johnson and his associates (Johnson, Goldstein, & Dudraine, 1979) found that most heroin addicts do not take heroin every day. They also reported considerable variation in daily dosages. Stimson and Oppenheimer (1975) reported that two thirds of a sample of London heroin addicts had abstained for a period of one week or more since they became addicted. Bennett (1986) found that many of the subjects in his study reported periods of abstinence lasting months or years and that their daily consumption of heroin varied greatly: "Daily consumption was often variable, and addicts often voluntarily abstained for 1 or more days to manage their patterns of consumption" (p. 97).

We arrived at similar conclusions. On one occasion during our study, a police drug raid jailed almost every heroin dealer in an area of town where several of our addict-burglars usually "scored." For three days they were forced to search for alternative supplies and to buy from dealers they did not know and who did not know them. During this period, one informant with a $300 daily habit simply reduced his intake to "two papers" per day—about $40 in heroin. Others did the same. They did not appear to suffer significant physiological withdrawal symptoms during the short hiatus. We found that the most experienced drug users suffered the least. Although the more experienced addicts normally consumed a greater amount of drugs daily, they appeared to handle the drug shortage crisis better. They reported less sickness and fewer symptoms of withdrawal. One informant stated:

It's no big thing. It takes about three days before you get really sick. My bones hurt a little and I feel like I'm getting the flu. I can handle it.

He explained that he had suffered withdrawal many times and that the physiological symptoms were not as great as he had been told to expect when he was younger and less experienced. He said:

The first time you expect to get really, really sick. You always heard it was like dying. Since you expect it to be really bad, it is.

Other experienced addicts reported a similar ability to abstain or to reduce their dosage without severe physiological consequences. The consensus among the older, more experienced addicts is that withdrawal, although unpleasant, is not as painful an experience as most believe. Most told us that the more severe symptoms of withdrawal do not begin until approximately three days after cessation of use. The experienced addict does not panic into premature withdrawal symptoms. One female addict illustrated this point, stating:

I used to think if I missed getting a fix I'd get sick. If I woke up and didn't have a fix I'd start withdrawing. Get chills and diarrhea. Now I know it was mostly in my mind. I don't like to, but I can go two or three days without getting really sick.

It appears, then, that the pains of withdrawal from heroin are at least partially driven by psychological expectations. Addicts who have had considerable experience with withdrawal can better handle the physiological consequences than those with less experience.

The heroin addict-burglar appears to be more rational and more capable of self-regulation than previously thought. Under most circumstances the heroin addict's crimes are as rationally conceived and executed as those of a non-drug user with the same level of expertise.

THE COCAINE-USING BURGLAR

Cocaine users exhibited less ability to control their intake than did the heroin users we interviewed. Although it appeared that most cocaine users could skip days or even weeks between periods of cocaine use, once they began to use the drug they experienced a definite loss of control over their intake. Unlike heroin, which satiates the user after an appropriate dose, cocaine use results in a craving for more. The cocaine user is never satisfied (this is true to a lesser extent of the amphetamine user). Cocaine users frequently commit burglaries while under the influence of this stimulant drug, usually in order to buy more cocaine to satisfy the endless craving. Their crimes are frequently crimes of random opportunity and are often committed in a "smash and grab" manner. Cocaine users will not usually invest the time in planning and executing a burglary and are often not as subtle in gaining entry. They will kick down doors or break windows when less violent (and less noisy) alternatives are available. Cocaine and speed users are more prone to trash a house searching for property to steal. They will dump drawers and turn over mattresses in their haste. A burglary site that has been entered by kicking open the door or by smashing a window and then trashed by the burglar during the search for valuable items to steal is predictably the work of a burglar using a stimulant (cocaine or amphetamine) or of juveniles.

DRUG EFFECTS ON BURGLARY DECISIONS

One interesting finding regarding drugs was unexpected and, although reported previously (Bennett & Wright, 1984; Shover, 1971), has not been adequately discussed or analyzed. We expected to find that burglars committed burglaries to buy drugs. We had not expected to find that burglars also used drugs to initiate and facilitate the commission of their burglaries. Twenty-eight informants stated that, when possible, they fixed or "got high" before entering a target site. They referred to the need to "be steady" or to "keep up my nerve." Although perhaps a placebo effect, most concluded that they were better burglars when under the moderate influence of drugs or alcohol. Some reported enhanced vision and more acute hearing while under the influence of marijuana. Others perceived themselves to be more efficient, to act faster and with more decisiveness, while using cocaine. A larger group, over one half of the informants, reported that they drank alcohol, fixed, or smoked marijuana to overcome the fear brought on by the act of entering the target site. The drugs used to deal with fear were primarily central nervous system depressants. With only two exceptions, even the informants whose regular drug of choice was a stimulant, such as cocaine or "speed" (methamphetamine), used depressant drugs immediately before a burglary to lower anxiety and reduce fear, thus facilitating the criminal event. Many stated that without drugs or alcohol they would not have the courage to initiate the act or to stay in the residence long enough to search for and locate the items to steal. Further, they believed that without a calming drug they tended to overlook important environmental cues related to risk, as well as items hidden in the house that they otherwise would find. Åkerström (1983) reported a similar finding:

> Quite a few used either narcotics or alcohol in order to get the necessary confidence or courage. . . . One can thus conclude that since courage is such an important aspect, it will lead some criminals to use drugs before they commit crimes. (p. 21)

Drugs and Emotional Arousal

Research on the effect of emotion on cue utilization suggests that *emotional arousal* acts to reduce the range of cues that an organism responds to and that performance is either improved or impaired depending on the nature of the task involved. The range of cue utilization is the total number of environmental cues that an organism observes and to which it responds (Easterbrook, 1959). As the level of arousal is increased, cue utilization is decreased. Emotional arousal increases when experiencing general excitement, when under stress, or in threatening situations. Zajonc (1965, 1980) found that for individuals with high levels of arousal, responses to central cues were enhanced and more concentrated or focused, whereas responses to peripheral cues were impaired. Consequently, one might expect an increased ability to perform more automatic behavior patterns in high states of arousal when some task-irrelevant cues are neglected. However, such dominant responses may be inappropriate for situations requiring more creativeness and spontaneity, resulting in impaired performance. He described the phenomenon as a "funneling of the field of awareness." Reduction of the perceptual field, as caused by fear and excitement or the physiological stress of drug withdrawal, might therefore restrict attention to only the more salient cues. To the burglar, then, whose task is complex, a highly aroused state (anxiety, fear, stress) would be counterproductive, because to enter a residence, search for and seize property, and leave undetected, he or she must attend to even the most subtle environmental cues. Burglars must concurrently attend and respond to stimuli and events both inside and outside the burglary site, and to the movements and actions of accomplices, neighbors, passersby, and occupants. This type of attention requires what is referred to as *parallel processing*. Air traffic controllers, pilots, and short-order cooks, as well as burglars, must possess parallel processing skills.

Wayne, an experienced burglar, stated that he always smoked marijuana before entering a target site "to reduce the paranoia" and to increase his awareness. He stated:

I'm scared to death to go in a house. If I didn't smoke a joint or have a few drinks I couldn't do it. If you get inside and you're not "cool;" I mean if you're not aware of what's going on around you, you're gonna get caught.

Debbie, a heroin addict, stated that she fixed, when possible, before doing a burglary:

I'm so scared that I can't think straight without some "junk" or at least some "weed." Once I've got straight, then I'm OK. I'm not afraid and I can think good enough to get the job done and get away safe.

Jamie, a heavy cocaine user, stated he would never use cocaine before doing a burglary:

Coke makes you paranoid, man. If you're scared, then you don't need to get paranoid too. You get to running around on the inside of the house and you can't think right and you miss a lot of stuff.

By using depressant drugs or alcohol at an appropriate dose and time before entering a target site, the burglar may reduce the level of arousal brought on by fear and thereby possibly increase the range of cues utilized. To this extent, he or she may actually become a better burglar. There is, however, an optimal level of arousal for a task, and reducing or increasing the level of arousal below or above an optimal point may impair rather than increase performance (the classic inverted U-shaped dose-response performance curve). The burglar who reduces arousal to the point of nodding off, or the cocaine or methamphetamine user who attempts to ward off fear by using a stimulant such as cocaine or speed, impairs his or her utilization of both central and peripheral cues, and impairs rather than facilitates performance. Billy, a burglar who used marijuana and alcohol heavily, reported:

One time, man, I smoked some dope before I went in this place. I was already about half drunk. I found this comic book inside one of the kids' bedrooms and started reading it. I must have gone to sleep, man, 'cause the next thing I remember this cop was standing there shaking me and telling me to wake up.

STATE-DEPENDENT LEARNING

Drug-induced state-dependent learning is now a well-established phenomenon, and has attracted considerable interest in the past 20 years, particularly when humans perform complex tasks under the influence of drugs. *State-dependent learning* refers to the observation that behavior learned in one drug state is easier to remember when the drug state present in the initial learning is reinstated. Conversely, state-dependent learning is also observed when the behavior learned under one drug state is harder to remember when retention is tested in a different drug state. Consequently, state-dependent learning is often called *dissociated learning*. In a review of the literature, Jarbe (1986) reports studies using animals in which it appears that the animals were grossly amnesic of the initial learning if tested for retention in a different drug state. Generally, however, and particularly in studies with human subjects, decrements in retrieval associated with a change in drug state are partial.

In humans, alcohol, amphetamines, barbiturates, marijuana, minor tranquilizers, and nicotine have all been shown to produce state-dependent learning effects (see Lowe, 1986). If we extrapolate from laboratory studies to burglars, it could be suggested that burglars who repeatedly break into houses under the influence of a specific drug are developing a set of responses or techniques that are quite different from their technique under a different drug (or no drug). If learning the techniques of burglary under certain drugs is even slightly dissociated, this may be of considerable importance because of the widespread drug use among burglars. For example, consider the burglar who consistently carries out burglaries under the influence of cocaine. Although hardly a smooth professional with cocaine, one could speculate that if he or she were to engage in a burglary with a depressant drug, performance would be even less professional. This may account for the high rate of apprehension on the part of cocaine using burglars.

REINFORCEMENT

Using drugs before entering a target site not only reduces fear and increases utilization of environmental cues, it also reinforces the behavior. Operant conditioning principles state that behaviors that are followed by reward are more likely to recur than behaviors that go unrewarded. Burglary is rewarding (or reinforcing) in many ways.

Many informants reported that the planning and target selection process was a rewarding experience for them. Just as many persons enjoy planning a vacation or a fishing or hunting trip, many burglars also reported that planning a burglary was a pleasurable experience. Searching for a suitable target was also considered rewarding by most of our informants. For many the search was a social activity accompanied by drinking and drug taking. Rengert and Wasilchick (1985) reported similar findings. They described one informant's activities in the target search: "It was almost a game. . . . They enjoyed viewing the houses and almost made a game of predicting if anyone was home in the houses with desirable attributes of wealth" (pp. 37-38).

The actual break-in also has reinforcing characteristics. The informants almost unanimously reported a "rush" upon entering the site. Some referred to the feeling as a "rush of adrenaline." All found the feeling very pleasurable. The searching of the burglarized residence for items to steal was considered very pleasurable by all of our informants. Almost all of them described the feeling as one of excitement and anticipation. Several described the feeling with a statement similar to that of George:

I know that once I'm inside, everything I can find is mine. I can have anything there. It's like Christmas.[10]

A successful burglary also provides the participants with cash and/or property that can be converted to cash (or drugs). This is a powerful positive reinforcement.

The burglar is also rewarded through camaraderie with co-offenders after the successful crime. Just as golfers often replay the match afterward in the clubhouse, burglars frequently reported partying following a successful burglary, everyone retelling their own version of the activity. The recapping behavior is often accompanied by the use of alcohol and drugs, further reinforcing the behavior.

Reinforcement can also occur when unpleasant situations or states are reduced. This is termed negative reinforcement. Fear and anxiety, for example, are unpleasant states with internal physiological correlates (increased heart rate, blood pressure, perspiration, and so forth). Reducing these correlates through drug use immediately before the burglary serves as a reward and thereby increases the recurrence of both the drug use and the burglary behavior.

With both positive and negative reinforcers at work, and because burglary is among the crimes with the lowest clearance rates (little systematic punishment to extinguish the behavior), the behavior tends to perpetuate itself.

DRUGS AND TARGET SITE SELECTION

Target site selection, as opposed to the actual burglary, was just as often accomplished by our informants without specific benefit of drugs. This finding does not contradict the conclusion that using drugs may facilitate parallel processing and decision making while in the actual act of burglary; in fact, it complements findings on use of drugs prior to burglary to reduce fear. Selecting the target does not typically involve fear, stress, or other emotions that increase arousal and narrow perceptual awareness because the burglar is usually not at risk during the process. However, when burglars work in groups—with partners—even during site selection when they are not at risk many report an increase in arousal. They refer to this arousal as "psyching each other up." Drug use may reduce this arousal produced by the presence of others and enhance the target selection decision process. On the other hand, using drugs during the target selection stage when working alone could conceivably impair decision making. When little or no fear intrudes on the decision process, drug usage may produce a rebound effect and reduce utilization of both central and peripheral cues. This was illustrated during a ride along session with two informants, Ramon and Jesse, who usually worked together and who, when stable, were almost always in agreement about the vulnerability or potential risk of a target site. During this session, however, Ramon was very high on cocaine and Jesse was completely stable. Ramon rated each site considerably more vulnerable and much less risky than did Jesse. Ramon apparently did not consider (or perceive) a large, unfriendly dog in one yard, obvious signs of occupancy at another site, and neighbors outside next door to another site. One week later, when both Ramon and Jesse were stable and essentially equivalent in their intoxication, their burglary attractiveness ratings on the same sites coincided almost exactly.

Drug Effects on Burglary Attractiveness Ratings

During the staged activity analysis we attempted to determine whether the type of drug used (stimulant versus depressant) affected target selection decisions. The informants were asked to rate their drug state and to specify the type of drug being used at the time of the session. The burglary attractiveness ratings obtained during these sessions demonstrated significant differences between burglars using cocaine and those using heroin and marijuana, and between those using drugs and

Table 5.1 Burglary Ratings as a Function of Drug Type

The individual burglary attractiveness ratings (means) of burglars alone under the circumstances that actually prevailed at the time of the site inspection (now) and hypothetical circumstances for each type of drug whose influence the rater was under at the time of the staged analysis. The number of individual ratings from which each mean was obtained is given in parentheses. The results of one way analyses of variance comparing means across drug types are given below.

Drug type	At present (now)	Hypothetical Circumstances	
		Assuming no one is home	Assuming no one is home and $250 cash is inside
None	3.44 (34)	4.80 (25)	6.00 (23)
Heroin	2.17 (113)	5.13 (109)	6.42 (107)
Cocaine	4.41 (43)	5.79 (38)	6.54 (37)
Marijuana	3.00 (51)	5.41 (39)	5.54 (37)
	$F(3,237) = 6.33$ $p < .05$	$F(3,207) = 0.44$ $p > .05$	$F(3,200) = 0.58$ $p > .05$

a. For the *now* circumstance a subsequent Tukey's HSD test revealed the overall significant F ratio is attributed to the significant paired contrasts between heroin and no drug and heroin and cocaine, and between cocaine and marijuana.

those who were not under the influence of drugs at the time of the session. As shown in Table 5.1, heroin users gave significantly lower attractiveness ratings in the conditions that prevailed during the staged activity.

Cocaine users generally rated sites higher (more attractive) than did those who were not under the influence of drugs at the time of the staged activity and those who were using depressant drugs such as marijuana and heroin. Marijuana and heroin users rated sites less attractive as burglary sites than those who were not using drugs at the time of the staged activity. The trend was toward more cautious decisions on the part of those using depressant drugs and toward more risky decisions when using cocaine, a stimulant. Both depressant and stimulant drug users were differentiated from those who were not using drugs at the time of the staged activity—in the expected directions. Figure 5.1 illustrates the relationship between the type of drug used and attractiveness ratings assigned potential burglary targets.

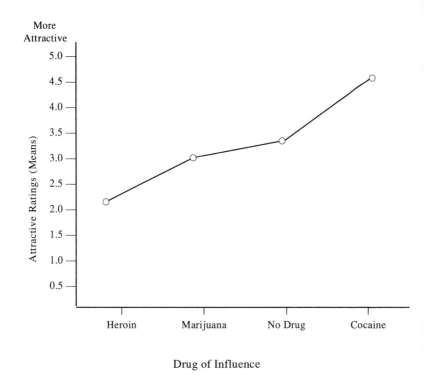

Figure 5.1 The individual burglary attractiveness ratings (means) of burglars alone under the circumstances that actually prevailed at the time of the site inspection (now) as a function of the drug of influence

Summary of Drug Effects

Our findings show that drug use and burglary are interrelated behaviors. Not only do burglars commit burglaries to obtain money to buy drugs, they also use drugs to initiate and facilitate the commission of their burglaries. Most of the informants in the study reported that drug use made them better burglars. To the extent that fear reduction, while under the moderate influence of alcohol or depressant drugs, facilitates parallel processing and allows burglars to be attentive to task-relevant cues in the environment, their self-reported improvement in performance appears to be accurate. This phenomenon may also be associated with enhancement of task ability attributable to state-dependent learning effects. The pleasure of searching for valuable items to steal, the intrinsic rewards from the proceeds of the burglary, the camaraderie of partying after the act, the reduction of fear through the use of drugs, and the failure of the criminal justice system to detect, apprehend, and punish burglars in any systematic way all serve to reinforce each step in the burglary process, increasing the likelihood that the behavior (burglary) will recur. Heroin-using burglars tend to be more rational, more professional, and relatively less likely to be arrested than burglars using cocaine or speed. The heroin user was found to have some control over his or her drug intake and appeared to be capable of desisting from or reducing drug intake whenever necessary. This finding has implications for crime prevention, as it tends to show that heroin users are not completely controlled by their habit and do not require a fixed supply of drugs each and every day. Crime prevention strategies might therefore reduce criminal activity and not simply displace it to another form, time, or place.

Burglars using heroin and marijuana rated sites less attractive than burglars who were not using drugs at the time of the staged activity. Cocaine-using burglars rated sites more attractive than did burglars who were not under the influence of drugs at the time or those who were using marijuana or heroin. These findings suggest that drug type may affect decision making by increasing or reducing central nervous system arousal, thereby increasing or decreasing the number of environmental cues utilized in the decision process.

CO-OFFENDER EFFECTS ON DECISION MAKING

One of the goals of the study was to determine whether the presence of co-offenders resulted in changes in decisions, particularly whether burglars took greater risks or were more conservative when working with partners. An increase in the extremity (in either direction) of the individual responses following group discussion is called *group polarization* (Shaw, 1981).

As shown in Table 5.2, there was a trend toward more cautious decisions by groups compared to individual decisions of members of the groups. Informants tended to view potential targets as riskier after group discussion. This is consistent with our decision-making model discussed earlier. When selecting a target, the burglar must contradict the assumptions that: (a) Someone is at home, (b) someone will see and report me, and (c) entry is too difficult. These assumptions are tested

Table 5.2 Alone Versus Group Attractiveness Ratings

The individual burglary attractiveness ratings (means) of burglars alone and with co-defenders under the circumstances that actually prevailed at the time of the site inspection (now) and hypothetical circumstances for high risk and previously hit sites as a function of day versus night staged analyses. The number of individual ratings of burglars alone and group ratings from those in groups from which each mean was obtained is given in parentheses.

	Alone					
			Hypothetical Circumstances			
Site/time	*At present (now)*		*Assuming no one is home*		*Assuming no one is home and $250 cash is inside*	
High risk/day	2.85	(60)	4.61	(51)	5.61	(43)
High risk/night	1.51	(59)	4.33	(55)	5.69	(55)
Previously hit/day	4.22	(59)	5.25	(48)	6.62	(42)
Previously hit/night	3.03	(58)	6.60	(53)	7.46	(52)
	Group					
High risk/day	1.89	(61)	2.24	(49)	2.07	(28)
High risk/night	.41	(29)	3.55	(29)	4.20	(30)
Previously hit/day	2.75	(61)	3.44	(45)	3.33	(24)
Previously hit/night	1.88	(25)	5.43	(21)	6.59	(22)

by the burglar by observing and attending to environmental cues that can contradict their validity. Our decision model suggests that the burglar need find evidence to contradict only one of the assumptions and the burglary is aborted, whereas he or she must find no evidence to contradict any of the three before the burglary is executed. It is probable that more eyes perceive more risk cues, which would bias them toward caution. We noted this while monitoring group discussions. In groups, the informants often pointed out risk and occupancy cues that had been initially overlooked by their co-offenders during individual ratings.

During the interviews, however, informants generally reported greater willingness to take chances and to engage in risky behavior when working in groups. Almost all of the informants stated that they psyched each other up, explaining that they were braver when working as a part of a group than when alone. The following statements are representative:

I wouldn't do [burglarize] this house by myself. I'd get some other people to help me. I'd be too scared to do it alone.

I'd have to have a posse [a burglary gang] to take on a place this big. No, it ain't something you'd do alone.

Man, you gotta get a bunch of guys together and build up your nerve to do a house in this part of town. You get a bunch of guys together and you psych each other up to do the job. If I got four or five people, I'd do any house out here.

These findings appear to be contradictory. It is possible they are yet another example of the disparity between what the informants told us they did and what they actually did during field simulations of their past crimes. Although they expressed the belief that they were braver and took greater chances when working in a group, the staged activity analysis showed them to be more cautious. We suggest that both findings are valid. The informants did become braver and more "risky" when working in groups; however, this tendency toward risky behavior was offset by their increased capacity (when in groups) to perceive and respond to risk cues at the target site. The net effect was toward less risky acts.

Social Facilitation

In animal studies of social facilitation, researchers have found that the presence of coactors of the same species increases activity of dominant or well-learned responses (Zajonc, 1965). In a classic study using human subjects, Floyd Allport (1920) concluded that the presence of coactors increased output and performance on well-learned responses but that performance in situations requiring problem-solving or judgment skills was impaired. Zajonc (1965, 1980) has suggested that the presence of others, either as spectators or as coactors, increases the individual's general arousal or drive level and may have the effect of either facilitating dominant well-learned responses (simple, well-learned responses) or inhibiting nondominant responses (complex, poorly learned responses).[11]

These studies suggest that burglars working in groups may tend to make errors in judgment and/or in technique, because of the increased level of arousal. These errors might contribute to a greater apprehension rate for burglars working in groups than for those working alone. The data support the hypothesis. All the informants reported a greater arousal level when working with a co-offender (psyching each other up) and their self-reported apprehension rate when working with partners was nearly five times greater than when working alone, supporting the hypothesis that performance is impaired on complex, poorly learned responses.[12]

Social facilitation studies also suggest that burglars working in groups could be expected to have a higher incidence of offending than when working alone. The data support this hypothesis as well. Several discussed hitting one house with one or more partners and then "going down the block," hitting several targets in a row.

Debbie confessed:

One night we hit this house here on the corner and then went down the block, hit 'em all. Once you get started, it's hard to stop.

Several others discussed burglary sprees, hitting numerous targets in one night or during a single time period. No solo burglar in the sample mentioned multiple burglaries during a single time period.

Summary of Group Effects

Group effects (by increasing arousal) increase the level of risk the burglar finds acceptable in a burglary situation; however, the burglar perceives more risk cues when working in a group, and thus may not act in a more risky fashion. Increasing the level of acceptable risk while increasing attentiveness to environmental cues appears to have a moderate net effect of a shift toward caution. This increased caution, however, is not reflected in lower rates of apprehension. Burglars working in groups reported an apprehension rate at least five times greater than those working alone. We believe that, although many factors may account for this finding, impairment in performance on complex tasks, which has been noted with other behaviors in group situations, may also occur in group burglary. Furthermore, the increased incidence rates that we found in the group situation also increase the number of times the burglar is at risk and, thereby, the apprehension rate.

6

Marketing Stolen Property

Any study of burglary must recognize the symbiotic relationship between the thief and the fence. Without fences few thieves could survive. The burglar's ability to market stolen property determines the success or failure of the criminal activities. Without someone to receive and dispose of stolen property, theft becomes a meaningless, profitless act. The fence fills this need.

Philip Cook (1989) concluded that most property crime is not the result of individual decisions of individual actors. It involves a number of actors with diverse roles engaging in a variety of activities that mimic legitimate business in many ways. The relationship between thief and fence is an excellent example.

The central role of the fence in property crime was recognized in the late eighteenth century by Patrick Colquhoun in his book, *A Treatise on the Police of the Metropolis* (1795). He wrote:"Nothing . . . can be more just than the old observation, 'That if there were no receivers there would be no thieves.' . . . Deprive a thief of a safe and ready market for his goods and he is undone" (cited in Siegel, 1989, p. 294).

The fence is the primary nexus between theft and the larger social structure, but research examining the interdependent roles of thief and fence is limited. Chappell and Walsh (1974) suggest that the nature of the act itself is partially responsible for the paucity of research. Fencing is a rational, businesslike activity with none of the traditional qualities associated with deviance. They write: "Lacking any obvious psychological difficulties, and remaining a well integrated participant in the socioeconomic structure, the fence could hold little interest for criminologists who were searching for more deviant personalities to study" (pp. 487-488).

Further, fencing is a crime with low visibility, conducted in great secrecy. Researchers have directed their attention to more visible crimes such as theft itself, or to violent crimes against persons for which statistics are available (Blakely & Goldsmith, 1976).

Much of what is known about fencing today comes from the work of Carl Klockars, whose book *The Professional Fence* (1974) is an exhaustive case history of a single professional receiver of stolen property. Other researchers, Chappell and Walsh (1974), Walsh (1976) and Steffensmeier (1986), have also concentrated on the activities of professional fences. Jerome Hall (1952) distinguished professional dealers from other criminal receivers by the intent to resell the stolen property and by the persistence with which they purchased these goods. Klockars (1974) elaborated on Hall's definition by detailing the criteria by which a professional fence might be differentiated from other receivers of stolen property. The professional fence, according to Klockars, (a) has direct contact with the thief, (b) buys and sells regularly and profitably, and (c) is a "public" figure who has acquired a reputation among lawbreakers, law enforcers, and others in the criminal community (p. 172). There is limited literature, however, on other levels of criminal receivers, and little reliable and valid data regarding the extent of fencing activities by nonprofessional receivers of stolen property or the degree to which the amateur fence contributes to the initiation and continuing support of property crime. Two studies have recognized the importance of this amateur class of criminal receiver. Hall (1952) included in his typology the *lay receiver,* who buys for personal consumption, and the *occasional receiver,* who purchases for resale, but on an infrequent basis. Stuart Henry (1978) studied property crimes committed by ordinary people in legitimate jobs. He concluded that receiving stolen property is not the province of professional criminals only, but is an everyday feature of ordinary people's lives. He states: "The artificial distinction between 'honest' and 'dishonest' masks the fact that the hidden economy is the on-the-side, illegal activity of 'honest' people who have legitimate jobs and who would never admit being dishonest" (p. 12).

During our research with burglars we became aware of a much greater diversity in the channels through which stolen property is redistributed than had been previously depicted in the literature (see also Henry, 1978). Our research indicates that a significant proportion of property stolen by burglars may be sold directly to the public—purchased for personal consumption or for resale.

In addition to ethnographic interviews with burglars and fences, we analyzed 50 police burglary reports in which apprehended burglars told police to whom they had sold their stolen merchandise. The following statements are representative:

(1) We took the microwave to [address deleted] and we sold it to an elderly Mexican lady for $30.

(2) I traded this stuff [cartons of cigarettes] to a man named Mario on the south side for heroin.

(3) The place where we took the guns was a house on [street name deleted] in Midland. A man named [name deleted] lives there. He is in a motor-cycle gang named the Outlaws. They buy guns.

(4) I asked my uncle if he wanted to buy the gun, and he asked me if it was stolen. I told him it was not. My uncle bought the gun for $25.

(5) I took Johnny and his brother-in-law to Frank's house. They did all the dealing with the man. I waited in my car while they went inside the trailer and sold him the VCR.

(6) I sold the disc player and the VCR to [name deleted] at [name deleted] Liquor Store.

(7) I went back to the lounge and found a man named [name deleted] and I asked him if he would buy the stolen items from me. He said that he would and he gave me $300 for everything. After I had sold the items to [name deleted] he told me that he was going to take the items to Mexico where he would sell them.

(8) About two weeks ago I met a man named [name deleted]. I met him through the wife of a friend of mine. She told me that [name deleted] might be willing to buy some stolen TVs I had from a burglary a few days before. I took the TVs over there and we plugged them in to see if they worked, and they did and he gave me $50 each for them.

Although these official report statements may not be representative of all burglars or their fences, they should provide some insights into the patterns of distribution of stolen property. The 50 randomly selected statements indicated that 9 burglars sold their merchandise to pawn-shops; 11 traded stolen property for drugs; 10 sold the items to friends or acquaintances; 10 sold stolen merchandise to strangers; 9 sold to employees or proprietors of otherwise legitimate businesses; and 1 used the stolen property as collateral with a bail bondsman. Although the number of official records analyzed is small, the results support the ethnographic data and suggest that the professional fence may have been displaced by a more diverse and readily accessed market for stolen property.

TYPOLOGY OF CRIMINAL RECEIVERS

Criminal receivers of stolen property are a diverse group ranging from professional criminals with ties to organized crime (Klockars, 1974; Steffensmeier, 1986) to respected citizens such as schoolteachers and businesspeople (Henry, 1978). They differ in the following characteristics:

(1) the frequency with which they purchase stolen property;
(2) the scale or volume of purchases of stolen property;
(3) the purpose of purchase (for personal consumption or for resale); and
(4) the level of commitment to purchasing stolen property.

These characteristics may be utilized to create a typology of receivers of stolen property. During the study we delineated three levels of receiver:

(1) *Professional receivers* are those whose principal enterprise is the purchase and redistribution of stolen property (Klockars, 1974; Steffensmeier, 1986). Professional receivers may transact for any stolen property for which there is a resale potential, or may specialize in stolen property compatible with their legitimate stock or legitimate business (jewelry, dry cleaning, appliance sales or service). The professional receiver generally makes purchases directly from the thief and almost exclusively for resale. These receivers were proactive in operation, establishing a reliable and persistent flow of merchandise, buying continuously and on a large scale, as well as providing strategic aid and organization for the thief's illicit activities.

(2) *Avocational receivers* purchase stolen property primarily for resale, but do not rely on buying and selling stolen property as their principal means of livelihood. Fencing is a part-time enterprise, secondary to, but usually associated with, their primary business activity.

We identified several categories of avocational receivers, including employees and proprietors of legitimate businesses who bought only items that could be assimilated into their legitimate stock, such as: (1) a laundry and dry cleaning proprietor who bought new clothing from shoplifters; (2) a truck stop owner who bought tools and tires; (3) a gold and silver exchange employee who purchased stolen jewelry and coins; (4) a videotape rental store proprietor who occasionally bought VCRs and portable color televisions; (5) a pawnshop clerk who accepted stolen guns; and (6) a liquor store owner who bought bottles of liquor and cartons of cigarettes.

A variety of other avocational receivers, although not purchasing stolen property with the frequency, volume, or commitment of a professional fence, bought any merchandise they could resell for a profit. Among these generalists were a tavern owner, a used furniture store proprietor, a gas station manager, and a tire store manager.

Another category of avocational receiver includes individuals whose primary occupations bring them into regular proximity with thieves. Such occupations may be legitimate, as with bail bondsmen or criminal defense lawyers. The primary occupation may also be illegitimate, as in the case of drug dealers, gamblers, or prostitutes. Because the nature of their enterprise makes it more likely that they will be offered stolen property, they may not have to cultivate a steady stream of stolen merchandise. In fact, these avocational receivers may operate from an entirely different economic perspective than other receivers in that they stand to lose financially by refusing to participate in the distribution of stolen property. This is particularly true for bail bondsmen and criminal defense attorneys, who may provide legitimate professional services to property offenders who cannot pay for these services with anything but stolen property (or the proceeds from their illegal activities). One informant, a bail bondsman, frequently accepted property he knew or suspected to be illegally obtained as payment or collateral for bonding services. Another avocational receiver, a criminal defense attorney, regularly accepted stolen property in payment for his services defending professional thieves. Thieves constitute a significant market for the services these receivers provide legitimately. To refuse such trade would eliminate these customers and seriously curtail earnings.

Street-level drug dealers may also accept stolen merchandise in exchange for drugs. Although not every drug dealer will barter for drugs, many find that fencing and drug sales are compatible enterprises. There are two apparent economic motivations for their willingness to barter: (a) bartering increases their drug sales, opening their market to those with stolen property but no cash; and (b) they can increase their profit margin by marketing the stolen property at a price well above that given in trade to the addict-thief. Informants consistently reported that drug dealers paid them as much as 50% less than did other outlets for their stolen property. One fence informant explained:

I know how to talk to a junkie. I can get it [stolen property] for nothing. I'll give them $30 or $40 for a VCR and can turn it around [resell] for $100.

The efficiency of the transaction—disposing of the stolen goods and obtaining drugs in one exchange—was for many addicts worth the reduced price paid by the drug dealer.

Generally, the avocational receiver is differentiated from the professional receiver by frequency of purchase, volume of activity, and level of commitment to the criminal enterprise. Avocational receivers do not rely on trade in stolen property as a major source of livelihood. Fencing is part-time activity.

(3) *Amateur receivers* may be defined as otherwise honest citizens who buy stolen property on a relatively small scale, primarily, but not exclusively, for personal consumption. Crime is peripheral, rather than central, to their lives. Like the shoplifters studied by Mary Cameron (1964), their major source of livelihood is from their respectable careers and they identify with the dominant values of society. Amateur fences are almost always initially solicited as customers and buy merchandise that is seldom specifically represented as stolen, although they may know or suspect that the property was not obtained legally by the seller. The amateur fence is often lured by a compellingly low price and a reasonable story to explain the bargain.

Amateur fences are also characterized by a tendency to disassociate themselves from the theft and, by extension, the victim of theft. They tend to perceive purchasing stolen property as victimless crime, if crime at all. Amateur fences tended to neutralize (Matza, 1964) their role in property theft by regarding their purchase as "simply a good bargain" or by rationalizing that the victim was an insurance company or another big business that "expects to lose a certain amount of merchandise." One amateur fence explained that she preferred to purchase new merchandise (usually from shoplifters) because the goods were more reliable and they did not have emotional attachments as they might had they been taken in a burglary. None of the amateur receivers we interviewed considered purchasing stolen property as *real* criminal activity. Most rationalized, "It was already stolen. If I didn't buy it, someone else would have." Although this may be an effective neutralization of the criminal characteristics of these transactions, it ignores the fact that receivers provide the economic impetus, if not the actual motivation, for theft.

One amateur fence we interviewed was a public-school teacher who began her part-time fencing when she was approached by a student who offered her a "really good deal" on certain items. She stated that the first time she bought something she did so to help out the student, who had financial problems. Afterward, however, the student began to offer her bargains regularly and she became a frequent customer. Eventually she began to offer her colleagues the opportunity to "get in on a good deal" and even posted a note in the teachers' lounge stating:

NEED A TV, VCR, MICROWAVE, ETC. ?????
SEE ME BEFORE YOU BUY. 1/2 OFF RETAIL.

She did not usually profit financially in this exchange, instead garnering the goodwill and appreciation of those to whom she afforded merchandise at well below wholesale prices. Although she admitted to the interviewer she "probably knew, deep down inside" that the items were stolen, she had not previously admitted it to herself. In explaining her motivation for purchasing goods in such an unconventional manner, she ironically described these goods as "a real steal."

Some individuals begin as amateur fences and advance in involvement as a result of the irresistible gains and virtually nonexistent sanctions of purchasing stolen property. The overwhelming increase in profits and the thrill of "beating the system" (or at least making a good deal) tempt them into increasingly active participation in the distribution of stolen property. One such amateur, a social worker, began her fencing activities when her husband purchased a household appliance from a thief he met in the course of his business as a plumber. At first their purchases were for their personal consumption. Later they bought Christmas presents for family members. They eventually established a thriving family business buying stolen property from thieves and selling it in garage sales and flea markets, as well as to a series of other amateur fences cultivated by the husband through the plumbing business. The informant advised the interviewer that she and her husband had put their son through college with the proceeds from their "part-time crime."

Although amateur and avocational fences do not purchase with the frequency, volume, or commitment of professional fences, our study indicates that they represent a large market for stolen goods, compensating for lack of volume with their sheer numbers (see also Henry, 1978). Interviews with burglars and shoplifters indicate an ubiquitous market for stolen property among otherwise honest citizens.

ADVANTAGES OF SELLING DIRECTLY
TO THE CONSUMER

Our findings reveal that many property offenders view direct contact with the public to be superior to other methods of distribution of stolen merchandise. It is difficult to identify stolen property under any circumstances, but distribution to the public, virtually hidden from law enforcement scrutiny, makes identification of both the property and the offender nearly impossible. Selling directly to the consuming public also has the effect of expanding the burglary "work force" for juveniles and drug using burglars. Juveniles and other inexperienced thieves face problems locating and establishing relations with professional fences. They may profitably enter the burglary work force only if they have access to the world of the professional receiver, or if they sell directly to the consumer. This second option appears to be becoming more common. Traditional fences also mistrust drug using thieves (Klockars, 1974; Steffensmeier, 1986). They believe that addicts will "give them up" rather than face a jail sentence and be without drugs. One professional fence interviewed during the study had a hand-lettered sign on his cash register stating: "NO ADDICTS."

Dealing directly with the consuming public has economic advantages as well, circumventing the tendency of middlemen (professional fences) to depreciate the value of the stolen property to sustain their margin of profit. Nor is the intent to resell exclusive to the more highly organized fence. A significant proportion of nonprofessional fences buy stolen property directly from the thief with specific intent to resell.

CONTRACTING FOR THEFT

Like the professional fence, amateur and avocational fences may also play an integral role in the organization and promotion of future theft. Contracting for future purchase has previously been attributed exclusively to the professional fence as a means of exercising control over the nature and quantity of their stolen goods inventory (Shover, 1971). We found, however, that amateur and avocational fences frequently contract for specific items to be purchased in the future.

One burglar described a dialogue in which such a transaction occurred:

CITIZEN: I'm looking for a nice diamond for my wife. About one carat—
              something nice. Can you get something like that?
BURGLAR: I'll keep my eyes open. How much you want to pay?

In this exchange the prospective receiver contracts for the purchase of a diamond and establishes the criteria of size, quality, and price. Contracting for purchase affords the buyer control over the merchandise to be purchased, and the thief benefits by establishing a ready market and price in advance. The thief may then steal a diamond himself or herself, or may act as a broker for another thief or another receiver and take a fee for this service. In either case the receiver, not the thief, initiated the crime.

In another instance, a criminal defense attorney agreed to represent a burglar in a criminal prosecution, telling the client that he wanted a gold Rolex as his fee. He later proudly displayed the watch to the interviewer, saying, "This is a special order."

Avocational and amateur receivers may also take an active role in the theft by providing offenders with information about potentially lucrative targets for burglary in the same way professional receivers do. The avocational receiver might even have greater access than the professional fence to strategic information regarding potential victims; their possessions, schedules, and security precautions. We discovered two avocational receivers who contracted for theft and facilitated its execution to obtain some specific item. These receivers, a gunsmith and a property appraiser, acquired specialized and intricate knowledge of certain types of valuable property while engaged in their legitimate enterprises. Such information frequently included the value, location, and security precautions for the property, as well as detailed insights into the habits and routines of the owners. One informant reported that his contact in such an arrangement would further minimize the risk (and maximize a successful theft) by arranging for the owner of the property to be out of town at the time specified for the burglary.

SUMMARY

The burgeoning increase in property theft in the past decade may reflect the development of a more pervasive marketplace for stolen goods. Although the literature indicates that most stolen property is purchased from the thief by professional fences, our findings reveal that the marketplace for stolen property is both diverse and ubiquitous. Amateur and avocational fences, purchasing for resale and for personal consumption, may purchase and redistribute as much as 60% to 70% of all stolen property. We located and interviewed both professional and nonprofessional receivers, including schoolteachers, social workers, plumbers, operators of small business establishments, attorneys, bail bond agents, drug dealers, systems analysts, college professors, high school and college students, and other individuals who regularly or occasionally purchased merchandise they knew or believed to be stolen. Seldom did these individuals perceive themselves to be criminals. They rationalized their activities as merely "good business," or justified their activities with statements such as, "It was already stolen. If I don't buy it, someone else will."

In much the same fashion as professional fences, amateur and avocational fences also contribute to future criminal activity by contracting for the purchase of specific items, occasionally even providing the thief with strategic information such as location of a particular item, security arrangements at the site, and the schedule of the owners or guardians.

There is a clear need to recognize the implications of this new and diverse market for stolen property. Traditional law enforcement strategies may be even less effective than before in reducing and controlling property crime.

7

Terminating a Criminal Career

A pattern of desisting from crime or engaging in less serious crimes was observed among the older, more experienced burglars and on the part of many who were interviewed but did not qualify as informants because they had retired or had reduced their activity level below that required by our operational definition of active burglars. Four of our informants were *desisters* at the time of the study. They had either terminated their criminal careers completely or had switched from burglary to "less serious" offenses such as shoplifting or fencing. Most of the remaining 26 informants had desisted at least once during their criminal careers.

DESISTING FROM CRIME

Desistance has been a controversial topic in criminology.[13] Research has generally shown a decline in criminal activity as the individual ages (Cohen & Land, 1987; Glassner, Ksander, Berg, & Johnson, 1983; Hirschi & Gottfredson, 1983; Wilson & Herrnstein, 1985; Wolfgang, Figlio, & Sellin, 1972). Some criminologists conclude that age is a constant and that crime rates decline steadily after peaking in the early adult years. Hirschi and Gottfredson (1983), the champions of this position, argue that age does not interact with other variables and has a direct effect on crime rates. It is a variable independent of other variables. This age-crime curve is consistent over time, space, and culture.

Others suggest that there are social factors associated with age such as employment, education, life-style, peer relations, social control, and marriage that explain the "aging-out" phenomenon. From this perspective, Siegel (1989) asserts, "Crime would then be conceived of as a type of social event that takes on different meanings at different times in a person's life" (p. 73).

Farrington (1986) and Blumstein and his associates (Blumstein, Cohen, & Farrington, 1988) maintain that persons begin to specialize in certain criminal activities as they age and neither the frequency nor the type of an individual's criminal activity is constant. This position advocates studying criminality as a career, undergoing evolving patterns or cycles in a person's lifetime. For instance, Steffensmeier and his associates (Steffensmeier, Allen, Harer, & Streifel, 1987) found that although the rates for some crimes decline with age, others such as fraud, embezzlement, and gambling are less likely to decline with maturity.

Other age-related factors are associated with criminality. Greenburg (1985) and Farrington (1986) have shown that a person who begins criminal patterns at an early age and who gains an official record is more likely to continue in criminal activity.

Despite the controversy over how age is related to crime, there is little doubt that crime rates decline with age. There are a number of explanations for the aging-out phenomenon.

Trasler (1987) suggests that crime by youths is exciting and fun and provides adventuresome social activity in an otherwise boring and unsympathetic world. As they grow older their life patterns are inconsistent with crime—they literally grow out of crime (Siegel, 1989).

Wilson and Herrnstein (1985) present an explanation that is closely linked to socialization. Adolescent deviance is associated with the need for conventionally unattainable money and sex and reinforced by peers who defy conventional morality. Their energy and strength, combined with a lack of economic skills and with relationships with peers, create the conditions favorable to crime. As the individual matures the small gains from petty crimes lose their attractiveness and legitimate sources of money, sex, alcohol, and status become available. In addition, adulthood brings powerful ties to conventional society, including jobs and acquisition of a family. Adult peers usually espouse values that are in opposition to risk taking and law violation (Siegel, 1989).

Charles Tittle (1988) maintains that aging out of crime is more a matter of interpersonal relationships than of any emotional or physical process. He suggests that children who get into trouble early in life and are labeled by authorities as troublemakers may have little choice but to pursue a criminal career (Siegel, 1989). Even these individuals will eventually slow down. Crime is too physically demanding, too dangerous and emotionally taxing—the punishments too harsh and long lasting—to be a way of life for most people.

Another view considers desistance to be associated with the fear of punishment. Glassner et al. (1983) associates aging out of crime to the knowledge by youth that once they have reached the age when they become subject to the jurisdiction of adult courts and penal institutions, punishment will be decidedly harsher.

FINDINGS

Among the desisters in our study, the decision to desist—to abandon a career as a burglar—often appeared to be the result of reappraisal of the costs and benefits of a criminal life-style. This reappraisal appeared to begin in the late 20s and early 30s for most of those we interviewed. In one case the burglar was over 40 years of age before deciding that life as a burglar was "too hard." In another, the burglar was only 19 years of age when he made the decision to desist.

We found support for most of the aging-out theories among our informants. It appeared that the decision to desist or to substitute one criminal activity for another was an individual decision. For one, marriage and the acquisition of a family appeared to be the primary motivation. For others, desistance was a gradual process that appeared to be associated with the disintegration of the adolescent peer group, and with employment and the ability to earn money legitimately.

For most of the desisters we interviewed, however, the final decision to terminate a criminal life-style was primarily the result of their increasing fear of punishment. In the early years of their criminal career, the informants stated that they did not perceive the criminal justice system as a deterrent to their criminal activities. The risk-gain calculus they employed when making decisions about criminal activity placed little weight on the probability of official sanctions. They were aware of the low apprehension rate for property crimes and believed the probability of being arrested for any specific crime was very small. Each active informant was asked, "For any particular burglary, what do you think are your chances of being caught?" Over 90% of the informants replied either "1 in 50" or "1 in 100." Their own arrest history confirmed and reinforced this perception. Thus arrest appeared to be a negligible factor in their cost-benefit analysis.

Furthermore, most believed that even if they were arrested and convicted, they would be granted probation for the first conviction for burglary or other property crime. As one informant stated, "You get one free crime." The perception of probation as a free crime was widespread. As a sanction, probation was perceived as a suspended sentence with almost no negative consequences. The informants we interviewed regularly committed crimes and used drugs while on probation—and parole. Few of them felt any serious pressure to cease or even reduce their criminal activities during their probationary period. The general perception was that probation and parole officers were overworked, understaffed, and underfunded. The informants were asked if they had been required to submit to random drug screening during their term of probation or parole. Over 75% of those who were on probation or parole, or had previously been on probation or parole, stated they had not. Several stated that the probation or parole officer scheduled urine screening tests as much as 30 days in advance. This had the practical effect of allowing the probationer to "get clean" for the test or to avoid the test altogether. Most, however, had never been required to submit a urine sample for drug screening purposes. Others avoided urine testing by failing to show for scheduled tests or failing to make their regular report day whenever they suspected or were told by other probationers to expect a surprise urine screening. Few reported serious consequences as a result of their artifice. Probation officers were thought by the informants to be too busy to follow up on these evasions.

Although the risk side of the equation was perceived to be negligible because of the inadequacy of the criminal justice system, the gain or benefit side was enhanced by the excitement of crime, the monetary benefits of crime, and the association of crime and drug use (viewed as a pleasurable experience by most informants). Operant conditioning theory demonstrates that behaviors that are rewarded (reinforced) tend to recur and behaviors that are punished are suppressed. To be effective as a suppressor, however, punishment must be immediate, reasonably severe, and consistent.

Burglary provides many reinforcements to the participants. Our informants related numerous reward points during and after a burglary (see Chapter 5, "Reinforcement"). On the other hand, punishments are few and intermittent. Burglars consistently reported committing 50 to 100 crimes before being apprehended and two to three times that many between periods of incarceration. Thus, whenever the cost-benefit analysis was employed, the gains and benefits were perceived to outweigh vastly the possible risks. However, like the subjects studied by Glassner and his associates (1983), there was a point in the careers of our informants at which the costs/risks appeared to be weighted more heavily. Although those who had served a short term of imprisonment (a year or less) did not often view the experience as particularly onerous, those who served longer sentences (defined by almost all as three to five years or more) felt the pains of imprisonment more surely. Many felt they could serve a year or two easily, but beyond that, the time was too "hard to do." One 43-year-old former burglar stated:

I can still do six months in county or even a year in the joint, but as I get older the time gets harder and harder to do. Didn't used to be. I could do a nickel [five years] with no sweat. Can't no more.

Another told us:

A year ain't no time. I can do that. I don't want to take no chances on having to serve five or six or seven years. That's more than I could do.

The pattern of desisting from crime or changing their predominant criminal activity to one less physically demanding or one with less harsh penalties was most readily apparent in the careers of those informants who had served at least one previous incarceration and who perceived that the next conviction might carry a substantially longer term of imprisonment. Recent research appears to support this observation. In a study of 108,000 persons released from prisons in 11 states in 1983, the Bureau of Justice Statistics reported that prisoners who had served more than five years in prison had lower rates of rearrest than other offenders (Beck, 1989).

Arturo, a desister for the past three years, told us that not only would the sentences be longer because of his past record, he would be placed in a more secure institution and would have difficulty making parole:

Automatically they would send me to a maximum security unit. The possibilities would be slim, because of my label [recidivist], that I would make parole.

The informants also perceived that the certainty of apprehension, conviction, and punishment increased after the first incarceration. Previous research on the deterrent effects of certainty and of severity of sanctions has found certainty to be more important than severity in producing conformity (Hawkins & Alpert, 1989; Tittle & Logan, 1973; Zimring & Hawkins, 1973). Tittle and Logan (1973) concluded that severity is associated with lower crime rates only at certain levels of certainty. Data from the present study appear to support this hypothesis. Severity of punishment has little, if any, impact on the risk-gain calculus of the younger offender—until the probability of punishment becomes greater. The probability of being apprehended for a crime was judged by our informants to be greater as they became better known to the police. They believed that their modus operandi was more often recognized and that they were more likely to be considered possible suspects after a crime. Previously incarcerated burglars also viewed themselves as more likely to be convicted if apprehended. Prosecutors were perceived to be more likely to indict and go to trial in the case of a recidivist or to use previous convictions as leverage in plea bargaining. Previously convicted burglars are thus more likely to plead guilty and negotiate a sentence, knowing that if they go to trial and are convicted, the sentence will be much longer than one negotiated in advance. Benny, a journeyman burglar with two previous incarcerations, told us why he eventually gave up crime:

It got to where they come and got me every time something went down within five miles of my house. I was afraid of getting 40 years or life or something.

Åkerström (1983) reported a similar finding: "The former thieves I have talked to often referred to the fact that at the end of their careers, they got caught too easily due to their records and the time inside tended to increase" (p. 203).

When long sentences began to seem inevitable, many of the older, recidivist burglars in our study desisted or took up less serious crime. Some reported getting out of the criminal life entirely, or trying to. One informant told us:

I've been down twice before and the next one could be the "bitch" [life imprisonment as a habitual offender]. It's not worth it anymore.

A larger group reported that they began to participate in less serious crimes. Fearing the consequences of a new felony conviction, many began shoplifting—boosting—a misdemeanor in most jurisdictions. Arturo said:

I didn't want to get the bitch so I quite doing burglaries and started shoplifting.

Arturo, like many other burglars turned boosters, found that merchandise obtained through shoplifting is more easily converted to cash and more profitable than items obtained through burglary. Shoplifted items are new and usually have a price tag attached. They are easy to fence and the price is usually better than for used items taken in a burglary. Shoplifters can also attempt to obtain a refund from the store when the items were stolen, thus recouping 100% of the value instead of the 30% to 50% that they would receive from a fence. A conviction for shoplifting is also less likely to result in a prison sentence than a conviction for burglary is.

This functional displacement into less serious criminal activity appears to result, at least partially, from the deterrent effect of fairly predictable apprehension, conviction, and longer sentences for previously convicted burglars, and from their perceptions of boosting as being a more cost effective, and less risky, mode of criminal behavior.

These findings may be an artifact of the sample selection or of the local criminal culture. Rengert and Wasilchick (1989) found that burglars who were displaced from their usual activities tended to engage in more serious criminal activity, such as robbery. If, however, functional displacement is brought about by an assessment of the costs and risks of burglary compared to the potential rewards, then displacement into more serious criminal activity would not be a rational response.

The decision to terminate a criminal career or even to effect a career change (shoplifting instead of burglary) must be considered in relation to drug use by the offenders. All of our informants were drug addicts or regular users of illegal drugs. Terminating a criminal career would almost necessarily be associated with a change in drug use patterns.

We found that the cessation of the criminal career and the drug use patterns tended to occur at the same time. We have previously proposed that criminal activity is rational behavior. The individual chooses criminal behavior after a rational assessment of the risks and costs of crime compared to the potential rewards. Bennett (1986) characterizes drug taking behavior as equally rational. He argues that offender choices and decisions govern in important ways the initiation, continuation, and cessation of drug use. He concludes that individuals desist from drug use for many of the same reasons as individuals who desist from other criminal activity. He concludes that situational factors such as a change of job or abode sometimes play a role in the addict's decision to desist from drug taking. Sometimes addicts simply tire of the life-style. In short, drug users are much more in control of their lives than previously thought.

The rational choice perspective appears, therefore, to be a useful way of understanding and analyzing not only the initiation of criminal behavior and drug taking, but also the cessation of these behaviors.

8

Implications for Public Policy

Crime prevention strategies based on rational choice theory assume that offenders freely and actively choose to commit crimes, basing their decisions upon a rational calculation of the costs and benefits associated with the behavior and arriving at a decision that maximizes gain (Bennett, 1986). Our findings support a *limited* rational choice model of criminal decision making and suggest that only in extreme cases are criminal events not characterized by at least limited rationality. The findings suggest that although offenders are not completely rational, they may usually be characterized as exercising free will in choosing among alternatives. Most burglaries, however, do not result from a careful planning process or the use of sophisticated techniques. Unlike the economic model of crime that relies on the concept of maximization of outcomes, our limited rationality explanation of burglary rests on the assumption that burglars are seeking satisfactory target choices, not optimal ones. The decision model can best be characterized as a satisficing (Simon, 1982) strategy as opposed to an optimizing one. We found that most burglars are opportunists and respond primarily to cues in the physical environment that indicate immediate vulnerability and immediate risk. These opportunistic burglars do not heavily weigh long-term costs, risks, or benefits. To be effective, crime prevention strategies must consider this here-and-now orientation of the typical burglar.

A burglar is more likely to respond to crime prevention strategies at the neighborhood, block, or individual residence level than to those at the community, state, or national level. Except under certain circumstances, crime prevention strategies at the community level, such as increased levels of prosecution, or at the state level, such as increasing statutory penalties for burglary, were not perceived by the informants as being as effective as micro-level strategies instituted by the residents of a potential target site, such as buying a dog or installing an alarm.

Our informants appeared to be more concerned with the possibility of immediate detection and with immediate rewards. Crime prevention strategies that assign the risks and costs of burglary to the future (after apprehension or after conviction) were viewed by most of our informants as almost hypothetical. With the exception of those burglars who had served one or more previous sentences the potential for future punishment did not appear to deter them to any significant degree, undoubtedly because if punishment is rendered, it is long delayed. Rewards from crime, on the other hand, are numerous and immediate.

DRUGS AND CRIME PREVENTION

Any attempt to reduce the level of property crime must take into account its interdependence with drug use. Traditional wisdom assumes that unless demand for drugs is reduced (through education and treatment), supplies of drugs are interdicted (through vigorous law enforcement), or the use of drugs is legalized, the level of predatory property crime will continue to rise. Our research suggests, however, the possibility that drug use does not create an intractable impetus to crime. If addicts can, as our informants reported, control their intake, then crime prevention measures might have the effect of reducing both property crime rates and drug use. Except for extreme cases of imminent drug withdrawal, addicts will be deterred by the same strategies that deter other burglars.

Our research revealed numerous instances in which an addicted offender planned a burglary and was deterred temporarily by some situational factor, such as a neighbor watching the target house or the presence of a dog or an alarm system. Occasionally the deterred burglar located another burglary target and committed a burglary, as intended. Just as often, however, the planned crime was not committed and the potential burglar borrowed money, shoplifted, or sold something legitimately obtained. From a public policy perspective, each of these alternative courses of action is preferable to burglary. This is not to suggest that supply and demand strategies should be abandoned, rather that situational crime prevention measures might serve as an adjunct to them.

Findings regarding mutual interdependence of drugs and property crime suggest that intervention strategies must target both behaviors. Drugs don't cause crime, they facilitate and reinforce it. Until the drug abuse aspect of property crime is adequately addressed, no intervention strategy will be effective in reducing the rate and incidence of property crime.

The research indicated that, at least in the jurisdiction studied, community correctional programs failed to screen property offenders aggressively for drug use. We believe that regular, random drug screening and drug treatment must be an essential component of any probation, parole, or pretrial services supervision plan. Most drug screening programs in criminal justice test known or suspected users only. Findings that indicate that two to four times more arrested offenders use drugs than are discovered by self-reports suggest that all pretrial releasees and all probationers be initially screened for drug use. In the case of new referrals, only when three to five random drug screenings have failed to show drug use should the screening requirement be reduced or eliminated. For those who are known drug users or those whose initial screenings give evidence of drug use, drug testing and treatment should be mandated for the entire term of supervision.

HINDERING CRIMINAL OPPORTUNITIES

Furthermore, the opportunity to commit property crime must be disrupted. Rengert and Wasilchick (1989) found that time was an important aspect in defining criminal opportunities.

> This is because specific sites are opportunities for burglary only at specific times of day when they are unoccupied or appear to the burglar to be unguarded or vulnerable. Burglaries require that the burglar's schedule and that of the victim coincide to leave the home vulnerable. (p. 85)

This means that if potential burglars are working at legitimate employment or attending school during most of the hours when most homes are most vulnerable (8:00 a.m. to 4:00 p.m.), their opportunities for criminal activity are restricted. The findings of the present study demonstrated that individuals could not easily hold a job and commit burglaries at the same time. Prime burglary hours are also prime working hours. We suggest implementation of sanctions that restrict the offenders' discretionary use of those time periods during which society is most at risk from residential property crime—the typical working day. Probation and parole conditions should mandate full *daytime* employment or some approved alternative, such as school or vocational training. Supervised restriction to the home (house arrest) might be required for those not working or in school.

Job training or full employment policies in probation and parole programs in the past have not proven completely successful. This may be the result of the belief that offenders would work at legitimate employment if they were given the opportunity or were vocationally qualified. Rengert and Wasilchick (1989) write: "Many assume that employment provides an alternative income source to crime which nearly everyone would choose if given the opportunity. Our research demonstrates that all the individuals we studied had the chance to choose work over crime" (p. 110).

The informants in the present study without exception possessed the necessary skills and the opportunity to maintain regular employment. They chose not to work. Their drug use, partying, and criminal behavior patterns were not compatible with regular employment.

MARKETING STOLEN PROPERTY

Cook (1989) has suggested looking to the economic paradigm as a means of analyzing crime. Marketing-oriented complexes of criminal activity undergird most forms of vice and theft. Therefore, it would be logical to apply this economic perspective in crime control—to develop a strategy to "guide the use of sanctions against the complex of activities that support a particular type of crime" (Cook, 1989, p. 68). Cook suggested that a thief-oriented enforcement strategy would be less effective than a comprehensive approach based on an understanding of the market for criminal activity. Any crime control measures that increase the cost/risk of doing business for the receivers of stolen property should reduce the profitability and therefore, ultimately, the volume of theft (Cook, 1989).

Law enforcement efforts in this domain are usually targeted toward the professional fence. It is true that targeting the professional fence may be more effective in reducing the incidence of theft than arresting several thieves. Thieves are "more readily replaceable" than those to whom they market their stolen merchandise (Cook, 1989, p. 70). We believe, however, that the professional fence represents a market for only 30% to 40% of all stolen property. Although professional fences exist and prosper, much stolen property is sold instead to ordinary, everyday, otherwise honest citizens. Stuart Henry (1978) wrote: "Taken together these property crimes are a significant feature of modern life, comprising a *hidden economy* operating within the legitimate economy of society" (p. 5).

The extent to which ordinary citizens participate in the hidden economy is yet undetermined, although our findings and those of Henry (1978) suggest that this part-time crime is ubiquitous. Unlike the professional fence, these individuals do not perceive of themselves as criminal or as part of the impetus that drives property crime and drug sales. Yet, were it not for their willingness to purchase stolen property, the market for stolen goods might well shrink to less than one-half its current size. Furthermore, given that recent research (NIJ, 1989a, 1989b) has found that 60% to 90% of all burglars use illegal drugs and use the proceeds from their thefts to buy drugs, the amateur fence might also be characterized as a facilitator of drug abuse and drug sales, as well as of burglary and other forms of property crime.

As Henry (1978, p. 13) states, however, "Members of the hidden economy are rarely caught breaking the law, and even when they are, they are rarely sent through the criminal processing mill. "The virtual lack of legal reaction and the carefree public attitude toward the activity and those who engage in it tends to perpetuate and expand the behavior.

We suggest that failure to portray and to respond to fencing activity as an inextricable aspect of burglary, theft, shoplifting, and illicit drug sales allows the amateur and the avocational fence to maintain a self-image of respectability--even of being sharp businesspeople. Henry (1978) concluded: "Crucially important to their participation in trading activities is whether they can excuse, justify, rationalize or otherwise preserve their moral character, should their activities be subsequently questioned."

The amateur and avocational fence utilize a variety of rationalizations to maintain their self-image. Among them are: (a) "Everyone does it," (b) "If I didn't, someone else would," (c) "I didn't know for sure that it was stolen," and (d) "No one was hurt but the insurance company." The failure of the criminal justice system to prosecute this part-time crime vigorously, or of society to condemn the activity, trivializes the behavior.

These relatively unstudied channels of redistribution of stolen property (amateur and avocational fences) may have important implications for crime prevention. Should crime prevention strategies circumscribe the market for stolen merchandise through prosecution of avocational and amateur fences, thieves would be forced to deal more frequently with professional receivers and would become more visible, because most professional fences are known to law enforcement. In addition, it is doubtful that the professional receivers would be able or willing to absorb the dramatic volume of stolen property currently being successfully redistributed through amateur fences. This market glut and the increased risks and costs to the professional receiver would probably lower the incidence of property crime. Finally, entry into the criminal work force by young and inexperienced thieves might be delayed or prevented if they failed to locate a ready market for their product.

Thus enforcement strategies targeting amateur and avocational fences could possibly decrease the incidence of property theft. By increasing the risks and costs to professional fences and the thieves with whom they deal, such strategies would serve as an economic deterrent to property theft.

SUMMARY

Our findings tend to support the general hypothesis that a rational, hierarchal, sequential decision-making process could not adequately explain a substantial amount of the variance in burglary. We agree with Zajonc's (1980) conclusions that decision making has aspects of both cognitive and affective processes and that a model of behavior must accommodate both. A crime prevention strategy that does not take into account the large percentage of burglars who use drugs and how drug use affects decision making, as well as the influence of coactors on the decision process, will be ineffective.

A cognitive-behavioral analysis of subroutines, one that takes into account drug and group effects within the larger template model, may serve as the most fertile paradigm with which to examine the burglar's decision-making process and to design and implement crime prevention strategies.

9

Reducing Vulnerability to Burglary

Findings from the study may also be utilized for the development and implementation of situational crime prevention measures designed to reduce the individual's probability of being victimized by burglars. The study found that although most burglars are opportunistic, they are nonetheless rational, making use of environmental cues at or near the proposed target site. Evidence obtained from the study suggests that even though there are no foolproof ways to protect a home from burglars, a few simple precautions will reduce vulnerability. These precautions are designed to modify the immediate environment to leave the impression of guardianship. This modification of the immediate environment is a form of situational crime prevention. The measures are particularly designed to thwart the opportunistic burglar—who represents about 70% of all burglars. They are designed to increase the risk to the burglar, increase the difficulty in committing the burglary, decrease the potential gain, and provide the illusion that the target site is occupied.

INCREASE THE BURGLAR'S RISK

Burglars fear being seen or identified and reported to the police while casing the neighborhood or committing the burglary. Consequently, the most effective prevention strategy is composed of "nosy neighbors," alert and vigilant persons who know their neighborhood and know the habits of those who live nearby. Nosy neighbors recognize strangers and know who has business being on the block. They exercise prudent guardianship by watching out for themselves and their fellow residents.

One informant, 23 years of age, who has been a burglar for seven years and arrested only once, told us that the thing she feared the most was "old people." She stated that neighborhoods with a predominance of elderly or retired persons were on her "no-hit" list. She said:

These people are nosy. They watch out for strangers and they call the police. I stay away from neighborhoods where old people live.

This female burglar expanded her no-hit list to include neighborhoods with children playing in yards and houses with noisy dogs. Children tend to be territorial, and they notice strangers. Occasionally, a youngster will walk right up to a stranger on foot in the neighborhood and inquire about the stranger's business or name. This is unnerving to the burglar casing a house and probing to determine whether it is occupied. Daytime burglars depend on being overlooked and will usually move on if they attract any attention. Noisy dogs are also unsettling. Dogs attract attention with their barking and they bark most often at strangers. They call attention to the burglar studying a potential target and cause the would-be burglar to feel less secure working in that neighborhood. Nosy humans and noisy dogs are the primary components of a successful burglary prevention strategy. This technique of watchfulness and guardianship, and reporting suspicious behavior to police, underlies crime prevention programs such as Neighborhood Watch.

Next to nosy neighbors and noisy dogs, the most effective means of increasing the risk for the burglar is installing a security system. We found that only the most professional burglars were willing to take on a house with a burglar alarm.

One of the most interesting findings of the research was the value of privacy fences—to the burglar. Most of the homes in the area studied had six- to eight-foot-high wood or masonry fences enclosing the backyard. These fences afford residents privacy for outdoor activities, and they allow the burglar the same protection from prying eyes. Replacing a privacy fence with a chain-link fence, or lowering the wooden fence to a maximum height of four feet, may be one of the best tactics an individual can employ to reduce the probability of becoming a burglary victim.

INCREASE THE DIFFICULTY FOR THE BURGLAR

Burglars follow the route of least resistance, almost always choosing a target that is easy to get into over one that appears difficult. Although it is virtually impossible to make a residence burglar proof, residents can make entry more difficult or more time consuming. One of the most effective ways to make entry more difficult is to install deadbolt or vertical-bolt locks and metal doors and door jambs. Findings from the present study and from prior research indicate that security hardware such as locks on doors and windows does deter many burglars. The burglars in the study had a general rule of thumb: "If it takes more than two minutes to get in, forget it." Although even the best locks and doors will not stop a determined thief, they are obstacles that require time and noise to circumvent.

The best locks in the world, however, are of no value if not used. Our informants estimated that doors and windows were not locked in over one half of all the houses they entered.

DECREASE THE POTENTIAL GAIN

Burglars are like short-term investors who weigh their potential gain against the immediate risks involved in the endeavor. Conspicuous displays of affluence increase an individual's attractiveness as a burglary target. Expensive jewelry, guns, art, and antiques on display in a home when repairmen, salesmen, deliverymen, and other strangers may be coming and going is an invitation to burglars who are constantly on the lookout for opportunity. Jewelry and other valuable small items, such as coin and stamp collections, should be stored in a safe deposit box. Publicity or casual talk about collections of guns, coin collections, or other hobbies might tip off a burglar that a home contains valuable items. The greater the potential payoff, the more risks the burglar will take to obtain it.

THE ILLUSION OF OCCUPANCY

The most important ingredient of a situational crime prevention approach to burglary is to give a residence the illusion of occupancy.

Nearly all (95%) burglars will avoid an occupied residence. The most important of all the steps the burglar takes in arriving at a decision to break into a targeted residence is to determine whether or not anyone is at home. There are a lot of cues that point to an unoccupied home, and vice versa. The traditional advice for residents leaving town on vacation is to enlist someone to pick up the newspapers and mail or to stop the paper and mail delivery altogether. That is still good advice, but it is not sufficient. Burglars look for lawns that are not mowed, the absence of the boat or cars from the driveway, and lights, particularly outdoor lights, kept on all day and all night.

The informants in the study suggested the following steps by which a house may be made to seem occupied.

(1) Install a telephone answering machine that answers within two rings and responds with either a message that implies that the resident stepped out for a few minutes and will be right back, or a message that implies that someone is home but the phone is rarely answered in person.

(2) Do not put a name on the mailbox or anywhere outside the home. Burglars often read a name on a mailbox, note the address, and simply go to a phone booth and get the number from the directory. They dial the number, put the phone down, and return to the door or window. If they hear the telephone still ringing, they know for sure no one is home. Permanent slot-type mail boxes where the mail drops through the door or wall, or U.S. Postal Service Centralized Mail Delivery boxes, are recommended over curbside boxes. They prevent the burglar from using mail left in the mailbox as a cue to determine whether anyone is at home and they prevent easy access to telephone numbers.

(3) Install inexpensive timers (about $20) on normally used interior and exterior lights so they turn on and off at normal times. An outside light left on all day or an inside light burning all night is a sure tip-off of absence.

(4) Put a radio or TV on a timer, too, and have it playing loud enough to be heard from outside the front door or window. Set the timer to play a radio from morning to bedtime. The TV is better in the evening. Put the TV in a room with a window to the outside and pull the blinds or curtains. An observer outside may confuse the flickering caused by the TV's ever-changing brightness with human movement on the inside.

(5) Leave a car in the driveway or in front of the house. As a habit, park it in various locations about the house from day to day. If away on a trip, ask a neighbor to move your car daily from one parking spot to

another, or to park his car in your driveway when coming to and from work.

(6) Ask a neighbor to leave a bag or can of garbage at your house on regular collection days.

(7) Ask a friend or neighbor to enter your house twice daily, once in the morning and again about dusk. It is a good idea to open the curtains, blinds, and shutters a bit in the morning and then close them in the evening.

(8) Install outdoor floodlights and have them on a timer, too. They should be set to come on before dusk and go off after sunrise.

In other words, even though no one is in the house, it can give the illusion of occupancy. None of these situational crime prevention strategies will guarantee that an individual will not be a burglary victim, but they should significantly reduce the odds of victimization.

APPENDIX A:

Issues Relating to Ethnographic Research in Criminology

Ethnography is particularly well suited for criminological investigation. The ethnographic design allows the researcher to observe directly the behavior under study and to determine how offenders themselves view their criminal activities. The researcher frequently becomes part of the criminals' culture and environment and gets to know them in their natural setting (Glassner & Carpenter, 1985). The rich detail and insights obtained from such research provide not only knowledge of the world and activities of the offender, but also insight into "how it is possible that such a world and acts exist, and therefore, how it might be otherwise" (Glassner & Carpenter, 1985, p. 2).

There is a large body of research that attempts to explore the factors taken into account by burglars in making the decision to offend and in selecting their targets. Many of these studies have been conducted in the ethnographic tradition: observing and talking to burglars about their attitudes, assumptions, perceptions, and beliefs, as well as the decision-making strategies and other aspects of their crimes. With limited exceptions (West, 1978) these studies have interviewed incarcerated burglars. Although some (Giallombardo, 1966; Irwin, 1972) conclude that there is much to be learned from interviewing incarcerated offenders, others are more cautious in attributing validity and reliability to data gathered from prisoners. One point of view holds that samples of incarcerated offenders are biased—in favor of "failures" at crime. Others doubt the veracity (or the memory) of the informants.

On the other hand, locating active criminals in the free world who are willing to be interviewed or observed in action is difficult and time consuming. If one can overcome this formidable barrier, however, the issues of validity and reliability of the data may be less problematic. As

Glassner and Carpenter (1985) contend, it is easier for potential subjects to refuse access than to lie about their activities. Furthermore, information gathered from informants may be cross-checked with other informants, with official records, and even through judicious contact with victims. In many cases, police officials may be able to support or refute certain information provided by informants. For example, an informant discusses a burglary he committed, telling the interviewer about the planning, target selection process, when and where the burglary occurred, how entry was gained, and what was taken. Some of those facts can be checked--when, where, and how the burglar entered and what was taken. If that part of the information is found to be accurate, then the other information (planning process and decision strategies) can be viewed as more credible.

The ability to check these facts, and yet protect the identity of the informants, depends largely upon the relationship established between law enforcement officials and the researchers. This requires pre-research negotiations and agreements between law enforcement agencies and the research team. In most instances, without such agreements and assistance, the research will either be impossible to carry out or will require much more time to complete and may result in less credible data. Some argue that cooperation between police and the research team may taint the study—and possibly subject the informants to criminal prosecution should they inadvertently become known to police through the process of validating information. Although this conceivably could occur, prudent planning can virtually eliminate the possibility.

ACCESS TO THE STUDY POPULATION

Not only may law enforcement agencies assist in cross-validating information gained from informants, they may also assist in making the initial contacts with persons in the criminal population sought by the researchers. Gaining entry and access to the desired criminal population (burglars, for example) is the most time-consuming and most difficult aspect of the study. McCall (1978) suggested that if researchers wanted to gain access to a criminal population, they should seek out persons (police officers, criminal lawyers, crime reporters, etc.) who might have contacts with the criminal population to be studied. Once introduced to a person in the proposed study population, the researchers may obtain other subjects through a snowball process of referrals.

SELECTING THE SAMPLE

In obtaining a snowball sample it is important to gain experienced and knowledgeable informants. A random sample is usually not possible. Carpenter and Glassner (1985) suggest that a purposive sample may be more desirable. Previous research has generally agreed that a relatively small proportion of the criminal population commits a large proportion of all criminal acts (Chaiken & Chaiken, 1982; Johnson et al., 1985; Wolfgang et al., 1972). The data suggest that this small group offends at a rate 10 to 15 times greater than that of other criminals. Thus one high incidence informant who has committed many crimes represents the experience (and knowledge) of several informants with lower individual crime rates. Therefore, it is important that the sample contains a significant number of these individuals.[14] The sample should be generally representative of the criminal population, however, requiring the inclusion of lower rate offenders, novices, and juveniles (in some types of research).

One of the sampling problems we faced during the study involved prospective informants who were not really burglars by our operational definition, yet who initially deceived us about their qualifications. Because of the snowball technique, we added new informants regularly. As the word about the research filtered through the drug-addict/criminal population of the community, some individuals perceived an opportunity to make a few dollars and enjoy a small scam at the same time. Although we were usually able to accept or disqualify a prospective informant after a short interview and/or after checking him or her out with other informants or through law enforcement contacts, a few managed to deceive us for a longer period. During a period late in the study we unknowingly snowballed into a group of "bottom of the barrel" junkies; heroin addicts who subsisted through petty theft, scams, and minor drug dealing. These individuals were long-term, heavy users. They were not, however, burglars. Several knew enough about burglary from previous experience, and from street and jail talk, to convince us initially to accept them as informants. Several such subjects were referred to us by an informant already in the study. She received a $50 referral fee for each and, as we discovered later, took one half of the stipend that we paid to the subjects she referred. After the second interview (Session 2) we began to be sure that these three informants were not legitimate burglars. During Session 3 we confronted them and they admitted that they were not burglars and were participating for the stipend. During the course of the study several other informants were found to have lied about their qualifications. Only one of the fakers was discovered before the second interview. We were merely another of the many hustles these drug addicts depended upon to survive. There is a lesson here for ethnographers studying criminal behavior. It is relatively easy for a generic criminal to pretend to be a skilled burglar—or armed robber, or drug dealer. Prison and jail house bull sessions and a lifetime of street talk have given them the ability to "talk a good crime." Only when the researcher actually goes into the field—into the social and physical environment of the subjects being studied—must the informant actually demonstrate any skills. From our experience, we believe that interview data gathered in jails, prisons, or from probation and parole populations may have serious validity problems (see our discussion in Chapter 2, "Rational Reconstruction").

In the present study, valuable information was obtained from recent desisters—those who had been career criminals, but because of aging, the increasingly lengthy sentences imposed on them as their career progressed, or other reasons had either given up crime as a life-style or had established new, less serious criminal activities (old-time burglars who were now shoplifting). These desisters were relatively easy to convince to become research informants because they were no longer "in the life" and in many cases had little to hide. They added a dimension to the research that was not often achieved by interviewing the active burglars. They could reflect, identify mileposts and turning points in their careers, and provide an overall criminal career perspective not available from those burglars at the beginning or in mid-career. We found that by reading transcripts of interviews with other burglars they could provide valuable insights, as well as a type of validity check on the data gained from the other burglars. One such informant, crime free for five years but considered by local law enforcement officers as "the most professional burglar ever to work this town," virtually became a consultant to the research team. Although he was never given access to the identities of the informants and he did not conduct interviews, much of the information obtained during the time he worked with us was filtered through him for comment. He would occasionally suggest new questions to ask or different avenues to explore with a

particular informant. He would also periodically suggest that an informant was lying about something and recommend that we confront the
informant about the inconsistency. Because he was almost invariably
correct in his surmise, we avoided gathering a lot of inaccurate data.

Including these desisters in the sample, although they were techni-
cally not active burglars, also gave us some insight into the process of
functional displacement—career changes by offenders. Most of them
had experienced one or more career changes. Most had tried a legitimate
job on several occasions; many had committed their crimes during both
drug-free and heavy drug-using periods, and most had tried their hand
at something other than burglary on occasion. Their perceptions of the
impact of age and imprisonment on the criminal career added an unexpected dimension to the research, a perspective on how burglars (and
presumably other criminals) may eventually desist from crime. Their
insight into the motivations, perceptions, and actions of the younger,
mid-career active burglars gave us a richer understanding of the phenomenon of burglary.

PROBLEMS OF LAW AND ETHICS

One of the problems encountered in most criminological ethnographic research, particularly that conducted in the criminals' natural
setting, is in obtaining valid data and observations without actually
breaking the law or transgressing the somewhat more vague boundaries
of professional ethics. These ethical and legal issues were particularly
important and relevant in this study. We planned to reconstruct (or
simulate) burglaries that the informants had committed and that may or
may not have been cleared. We wished to protect ourselves and our
informants from possible criminal actions and ethical disquietude.

We did not participate in planning or in discussing crimes to be
committed in the future by our informants. We advised them orally and
in writing that the promise of confidentiality would not extend to new
crimes. We asked them to discuss only crimes that had been committed
in the past. We justified our procedure on the basis that the crimes we
studied had already been committed, and that we had no involvement
in them whatsoever, except the knowledge gained later as to the identity
of the perpetrator(s). No one (including the victim) was damaged
further for our having knowledge of the identity of the guilty party. On

the other hand, if the knowledge we gained allowed us to suggest more effective crime prevention strategies, society benefited.

We were concerned with the effects of drug use (altered states of arousal and equilibrium) on the decision-making processes of the informants. We therefore conducted interviews and ride alongs (crime simulations or re-creations) with informants at various levels of drug arousal and at all hours. It was not unusual for one of us to be riding around town at 2:00 a.m. with two burglars who were high on drugs, or at 7:00 a.m. with a very sick heroin addict. We also faced the dilemma of having heroin addicts announce that they had to have a fix before they could go on with the interview and ask us to take them to their drug connection or to advance them money for heroin. We had previously stipulated that we would not loan money, make bail, or assist any informant if arrested. This proviso was a part of the oral agreement with the informants and was in writing as a part of the Voluntary Consent to Participate in Research that all informants read (or had read to them) and signed. When informants requested a loan we reminded them of this agreement and repeated that we were "poor college professors" who did not carry much money with us. We also told them (regularly) that the stipends we paid them were "government" money and that we did not have authority to loan or advance money. We did not want them to begin to think of us as potential robbery or burglary victims. This, for the most part, worked well. We did occasionally receive calls at home, at unusual hours, asking if we might be willing to interview them immediately because they needed money "to get their car fixed," or, in one case, "to get out of town in a hurry."

As trust and rapport developed between us and the informants some began to ask us to take them to their drug connections and wait while they got a fix. This began with a very articulate and professional burglar who was providing a wealth of information. He argued that he could not think straight until he got a fix and if we would just drive over to Alamosa Street (fictitious), he would go inside and be ready to complete the interview in five minutes. Not willing to drive a burglar to his drug connection and yet wishing to know how an addict's decision varied immediately after a fix, the interviewer compromised. He drove the informant to a city park two blocks from the address, dropped him off, and made an appointment to meet again in one-half hour. That seemed satisfactory to the informant. We used the same technique during the remainder of the study when such circumstances arose.

Several burglars tested the limits of the relationship by asking permission to smoke marijuana while we drove around re-creating past crimes. We refused permission each time. We offered to drop them off for a while (to let them smoke) and come back to pick them up later. This approach did not seem to trouble the informants or diminish rapport.

Because the informants were active burglars and continuously arrestable, we expected that the attrition rate would be 25% to 30%. We discovered, however, that we had considerably underestimated attrition. Over 75% of the informants were arrested for some crime at least once during the course of the study. At first we feared that they might believe that their arrests were connected to their association with us. Except for one almost disastrous incident, this did not seem to be the case. About midway into the study, at which point over 20 subjects were involved in the interview process, local police obtained 56 sealed indictments as the result of an ongoing "sting" operation. We lost several informants to arrest in one night. For a while after that there was a rumor going around that we were part of the sting. We managed to convince most of them that we were as unaware of the sting as they (and we were) and eventually retained as informants almost all those arrested.

In general, we were able to resolve most of the problems that arose by using common sense and by being consistently honest with the informants. Because the research was the first of its type, there was little precedent for guidance.

APPENDIX B:

Biographies of Selected Informants

The brief biographies that follow are generally representative of the informants in the study.

Robert

Robert is a professional burglar. He was born in Austin, Texas, in 1950. He graduated from high school in 1968 and was subsequently drafted into the Army, but opted to enlist in the Navy. He claims to have served two tours of duty with the Special Forces in Vietnam. He states that he received three Bronze Stars and a combat action award. When he returned home in 1973, he said:

It didn't mean anything to anybody and I couldn't get my old job back as a welder. Burglary was so easy.

He pulled his first burglary three months after returning home. in the years that followed he became a skilled and respected burglar. His specialty was lake cottages and vacation houses within a 90-mile radius of Austin.

Robert differed from the less professional burglars in our sample in several ways. First, his targets were always located far from his personal residence. Robert told the interviewer:

I take my van up to the lakes—sometimes a hundred miles from here. These houses are vacation homes. Sometimes the owner won't come back for a month or two, especially in the winter. I took air conditioners, everything I could fit into the van.

Second, he never had a mentor to teach him the trade of burglary. He told us:

The military taught me what I needed to know as a burglar. Planning, that's what I learned in the Army. Laying out a map in your head, getting it all together, and knowing who you're going to unload the stolen goods on before doing anything is also important. I guess my training in the Special Forces taught me to be sneaky and to rehearse things in my mind ahead of time because, you know, you're scared. The military taught me to have confidence in myself.

Finally, Robert was master of the ruse. All the burglars we worked with had developed probes to determine occupancy and the potential for the target site to be seen from other houses. Robert was an actor, having a varied routine to fit any occasion. Asked to describe examples of such probes, Robert answered:

Oh, I've got all kinds of ways to determine if somebody is at home. I might put on decent but not real outstanding clothes, and come out and do an acting routine. Looking down at my clipboard, I'd go up and knock on the door. I'm looking for a certain house, you know, and in case somebody is looking from across the street, I've opened the screen door with my foot to make it look like I'm talking with somebody. I'll move my arms half-pointing and say, "Okay, I'll go around to the back." Or, after knocking and nobody comes, I'll turn the doorknob. A lot of houses aren't locked. So I'll just walk in. Anybody who's watching thinks I've been asked inside by the owner.

Robert reported regular use of amphetamines, especially methamphetamine. He began injecting methamphetamine daily during his third year as a burglar. He stated that as he increased his speed use, he became sloppy as a burglar. He said that he was no longer professional about the selection of target sites nor about the distribution of the stolen merchandise. Once during this period Robert was high on methamphetamine and reported:

I'm talking about a house where there was a padlock on the back door and no vehicles around. Man, it looked liked nobody was there. When I got in I could smell smoke and I walked around. I opened the bedroom door to look in and see a fireplace going and a guy with this girl. I should have spotted that smoke coming out of the chimney and blown off the place.

Robert generally worked alone. There were occasions, however, when he needed help: either for assistance (to carry off very heavy items) or for "another pair of eyes" to watch for returning occupants. When he needed help he would invariably select a partner who had done "hard time" before, believing that such a person could not afford to be caught again. Robert also preferred partners on speed as opposed to heroin, saying:

A heroin addict will turn you in just to get his other shot, but a speed freak is not going to. He's too scared. A heroin addict you can't trust. A speed freak is too paranoid to turn you over.

Robert has recently reduced his drug use and has returned to professional burglary. He still uses speed; however, he claims to abstain when planning and executing burglaries.

Robert claims to have burglarized more than 2,000 dwellings during an eight-year period ending in 1981, when, after plea bargaining, he pleaded guilty to 51 counts of residential burglary. He subsequently served 4 years, 9 months of a 5-year sentence in the state prison.

Arturo

Arturo is a former professional burglar, having been "clean" for several years. He is 41 years old and is the oldest of five children. He began his criminal activity at age 14. Arturo's parents are still living and in their early 60s. Arturo's father no longer claims him as a son because of his past life as a criminal and drug addict. His mother continues to support him and wrote weekly during each period of incarceration. Arturo reports that his chief regret in his life is that his drug use and criminal activity destroyed his mother's life. He states that he is committed to straightening out, for both himself and to "make my mother proud of me for once" Arturo's father earned a modest living and the family was never on assistance. His mother never worked outside the home. Neither parent speaks English well and they live in an exclusively Hispanic neighborhood. Although Arturo dropped out of school in the ninth grade, he is intelligent, perceptive, and articulate. He attributes this to being a voracious reader while in prison with "endless hours without anything to do."

Arturo began his criminal career while in junior high school, primarily because of his association with a 16-year-old friend who had been confined to youth detention centers for various offenses. He eventually became a part of a group of five boys who did burglary and shoplifting. They used the proceeds of their delinquent activity to purchase alcohol and marijuana. Arturo didn't enjoy marijuana, however, and immediately began experimentation with speed, Quaaludes, LSD, and finally heroin. Arturo believes he became addicted after a year of what he terms infrequent use—only administering on weekends. His burglary activity increased to support his heroin habit. He dropped out of school and shoplifting and burglary became his occupation. Except for a four-month stint in the prison bakery he never worked in a conventional job. Arturo reports never being convicted as a juvenile, although he was arrested three times. Each time he refused to confess and was released as a result of insufficient evidence. As an adult, Arturo was convicted three times and spent a total of 13 years, 8 months in the Texas prison system. His first incarceration, for possession, resulted in a 7-year sentence. He served 5 years, 10 months. His behavior was erratic and netted him solitary confinement on four occasions. He was released and went to El Paso, where a friend and criminal associate lived. They began burglarizing and shoplifting. When the law "got close" on one occasion they moved to Mesa, Arizona, continuing their criminal activity. After a year they returned to Odessa. After being out of prison about 3½ years, Arturo was again convicted for burglary after a co-offender gave him up in exchange for a probated sentence. Arturo is philosophical about the incident. Although he asserts that he wouldn't "rat" on a partner, he stated that he was not in his "partner's shoes" and will not judge him. Arturo began his second incarceration with an aggressive, wild attitude and had long months of unpleasant physiological and psychological heroin withdrawal symptoms. Fights and failure to follow prison rules resulted in frequent and extended periods in solitary confinement. During this incarceration he read constantly and significantly increased his vocabulary, as well as improving his criminal expertise by association with other inmates. He served 4 years, 10 months of the 10 year sentence. Upon release, his aunts and sister paid to send him to a private drug rehabilitation center in El Paso, which, after three months, proved fruitless. He returned to Odessa—and his association with his lifelong friend and co-offender—and began a very active phase of burglary, check forgery, and fencing stolen property for other offenders. Arturo was notorious among law enforcement as well as businessmen and store security personnel. His infamy was so pervasive that he is still, after 10 years, not allowed in certain stores.

He remained "outside" for 2½ years, then was convicted on two counts of burglary. This third incarceration began like the others, but on his 35th birthday he decided he needed to "do something with his life" and had to get straight. He served 3 years of his sentence, receiving time for good behavior, and has remained clean since his release.

He is employed as a machinist, does volunteer work with drug addicts, and moonlights as a carpenter and general handyman. His association with all his friends and previous co-offenders has stopped, except for those who have stopped drug usage.

Donna

Donna is a white, 43-year-old professional criminal and heroin addict. She grew up in a lower-middle-class family. Both of her parents are living and are still married to one another. Her father has become moderately wealthy, having invested in oil leases and wells over the years. As a youngster her friends were "pimps, whores, and thieves." Donna dropped out of high school when she was 16 years old and married when she was 19. Her first and only marriage lasted five years, until her husband was sent to prison for armed robbery. Since she was 18 years old she has lived on the edge, supporting her marriage and herself through theft, burglary, shoplifting, and prostitution. She has "slowed down" over the past several years and now works occasionally for her father, who encourages her participation in a methadone maintenance program.

Donna's husband was 20 when she married him. She had never stolen until she met him. He served as her mentor in crime. They lived lavishly on the proceeds of their burglaries and armed robberies. She claims to have been "written up in the *Police Gazette*" during the heyday of her criminal activities.

She participated in her first burglary with her husband. She related:

The first one we did was a place out in the country. We knew they weren't there. I stood outside with a shotgun and I guess I would have shot rather than let my husband get caught. My job was to always stand watch with a shotgun.

In just the past three years she estimates she has participated in more than 200 to 300 burglaries—much more than she ever did when she was younger. She usually works with a male partner, but she breaks in, scans the rooms, and carries out as much as anyone. Sometimes she even works alone.

Donna likes to have inside information about the potential contents of a house before she burglarizes it. She states that she acquires such information by listening to people talk in restaurants and bars. She reports that she spends some mornings waiting at mall entrances/exits until a woman wearing expensive jewelry exits. She then follows the individual home. She reconnoiters the residence and returns later to burglarize it. She says:

So I drive by the front and back, looking for alarms that might go off. It was a lot easier over 20-something years ago. A lot easier. Just sit and watch. Then go up to the front door and knock. If no one answers, then go in. But back then, see, they didn't have all these alarms, motion sensors and heat sensors and stuff. When I drive by I pay more attention to the back—I look for a sliding glass door. If it doesn't look like it has an alarm setup of any type I'll come back that afternoon or the next morning. If the car is gone I go up and knock on the front door. Oh, if someone were to answer the door, you know, I say, "Pardon me, is Mr. Brown in? . . . Mr. Jennings?" Mister anything, anybody I know. If they say, "No, you've got the wrong house," I act confused and say, "I'm sorry, thank you."

During the 20 years that Donna has been addicted to heroin she has never been drug free for more than a two-month period. Even now, she supplements her methadone with one to five papers (about $20 per paper) of heroin a day. For a recent three-month period when she was *speedballing,* using cocaine and heroin at the same time, her habit ran $200 to $300 per day. In describing the many mornings when she'd wake up sick, having no heroin immediately at her disposal, she said:

Oh, I liked to use [heroin] before I would go and do a burglary, but I wasn't high, high, high, you know. I would have maybe fixed one or two papers to take the sick off then go to work [burglary]. You know, it's [heroin] a 24-hour-a-day problem. It doesn't go away. And then I'll go to work. But I'll do things that I wouldn't normally or ordinarily do when I'm sick. When I'm not sick, I'll stop and think a lot more. When I'm sick, I'll tend to hog anything I can, whether it be a house, a trailer. . . . I've gone into department stores and reached across the jewelry and watch counters and gotten stuff. I'm going to get it one way or another. I take greater risks when I'm sick.

When things got "too hot" for burglary Donna would turn to shoplifting—boosting. She had developed a reputation as a formidable booster, such that each Christmas season people would come to her with their requests. She'd carry a notebook and fill their Christmas shopping lists. Donna commented:

Now, because they're due so much hard time for burglary and stuff, you'll find a lot of professional burglars that are tired of doing hard time and so a lot of them are into boosting. But you need customers for that, because, well, say you go into a department store for instance. You go in there and just start grabbing and then you have to drive around everywhere to unload it. You got to have some people that want that stuff and want it now. I'll fill your order whether it's a dress, a camera, a Rolex, or a carton of cigarettes!

Donna also turns to boosting when she is extremely sick. Boosting is preferred during such times because it's a quicker way to get cash or turn merchandise for drugs:

You can run into a convenience store, get four cartons of cigarettes and you've got a "paper." Or you can go into any supermarket and get five or six packages of ribeye steaks. I can unload the steaks in 10 minutes.

Gerald

Gerald is 22 years old and a journeyman burglar. He was born in El Paso, Texas. Gerald's criminal life began early. He was 11 years old and living in Roswell, New Mexico, when his father left home. Soon afterward he broke into a neighborhood house with three other boys— all 11 years of age. They stole jewelry and money. The boys soon discovered there was money in burglary and decided to ride their bikes to what they called the "rich part of town." The four of them rode to the north side of town and hid their bikes in a field near a middle-class housing area. They walked for several blocks, finally finding a house that looked empty and burglarized it. Gerald commented retrospectively:

We did it, got away with it and liked it. We thought it was great. We spent the money on video games.

In that first year, Gerald and his friends broke into 15 to 20 homes; always at night. They always traveled by bicycle, but if the stolen merchandise was larger or heavier than they could carry on a bike, they would hide it and come back the next day in an older friend's car and pick it up.

When Gerald was 16 he was coached by two friends who were 18. They showed him how to disconnect alarms, open sliding patio doors, and other "tricks of the trade." The mentors only burglarized during the daytime. They taught Gerald how to sit patiently and "scope out a house," noting the time people left and returned and the whereabouts of others in the neighborhood. Gerald would sit in his car up the street about a half-block and just watch. He was breaking into up to three houses per week during one period with his older friends.

Gerald was 9 years old when he first experimented with marijuana, but it wasn't until he was 14 years old that he became a frequent user. He reports that after age 16, he was always high on marijuana when he did burglaries. To this day he continues to get high on marijuana before breaking into a house or apartment. Gerald commented:

When I'm on that high I don't worry about no fear. I don't have no fear in me. I feel more calmed about myself and I can think pretty clear when I'm high.

At 18, Gerald began using cocaine once or twice per week. He used cocaine in addition to marijuana and alcohol. He prefers *primos*, marijuana joints sprinkled with cocaine.

Gerald was most active as a burglar between the ages of 18 and 19. During this period he committed burglaries mostly to obtain money to buy cocaine. He states that before cocaine, he did burglaries to party and to support his car and girlfriends. Although Gerald claims never to be anything more than a weekly user of cocaine, obtaining it appears to have driven many of his burglaries.

Jerry

Jerry is black, the oldest son of a family of five children. Born and reared in west Texas, he is the best educated of all our burglars. He lacks a year's worth of senior credits toward a bachelor's degree in business administration. His father left the family when Jerry was 14 years old. His mother continued working as a maid but could barely make ends meet. Jerry is a heroin addict. He began as a burglar when he was 18 years old, just after graduating from high school. He learned the essential skills of a burglar from a friend who was 18 years old and always seemed to have a lot of money. Jerry liked the way he was doing things, and just "took up with him." This friend began showing Jerry what he had been doing to get money. At first, Jerry stood watch at target sites. Usually they'd enter through the rear alley and either jump the backyard fence or merely open the back gate. Jerry would watch the front street from the side of the house, just behind the fence. Jerry stated:

I'd get to where I could see the street and where my buddy could hear me. When we got in the house we would open the back door so we could have a way out. I'd watch. If I saw someone coming I'd go to the door and call him. I'd either whistle or holler and he would come out. If he needed me to help him with something heavy he would call me and I would go in. Most people will not come through the alley. Policemen won't come through the alley unless there was a report. So you don't have to watch the alley. They just patrol the streets; most of the time just the main streets. And if you watch them long enough you can tell which way they are going to go and when, 'cause they go almost the same way all the time.

Jerry and his friend continued doing night burglaries only, preferring the early evening. They burglarized houses in the neighborhood within about a one-mile radius of their own home. They claimed to burglarize only places where they knew the occupants and knew where they had gone. Thus they tended to know what was in the house.

Although Jerry's drug of choice during this period was marijuana, he reports never stealing drugs. He reports stealing "just for the money," and continues:

Anything you want, money could give it to you: cars, girls. You never keep any of this money. You never save any of this money. You don't, say, invest any of this money. The more money you make, the more you're just going to mess off.

After beginning to use, and becoming addicted to, heroin at age 31, Jerry began to use the proceeds from his crimes to buy heroin. He claims to have little disposable income now; instead he uses almost all of his money to maintain his heroin habit.

Jerry reported that he was always cautious to "fit in" a neighborhood. When casing an affluent white neighborhood, Jerry states:

During the day I have no reason to be there. If I could get some lawn mowers I'd have a reason to be out there. I need a reason to be there. At night I have no reason to be out there. That area, I stay away from. I work in mixed areas where blacks, whites and Mexicans would stay.

Jerry was married when he was 20 and soon afterward began a streak of four arrests for burglary for which he was not convicted. Then, when he was 21 he was arrested the fifth time. This time it was on 10 counts of burglary and 1 count of armed robbery. As before, the burglary charges were dropped because of a lack of evidence, but because he was personally identified in the armed robbery, Jerry said "I just couldn't beat that." Jerry spent the next five years in prison. During this period his wife divorced him but he took college classes and earned his

Associate of Arts degree. After leaving prison he remained in the free world for eight years, working primarily in construction and intermittently taking more college courses. He married a second time. At age 34 he was convicted and served another 5-year term in prison for delivery of a controlled substance. As with the first, his second wife divorced him while in prison.

He has been arrested for burglary eight times but never convicted of that offense. Presently he is on parole and continuing to commit burglaries and to buy and sell heroin. He is receiving a small monthly check from an insurance settlement. He stated:

I know it's going to run out sooner or later. I have a little extra money coming in too, and that's why I don't do much burglary now. 'Course, you don't have to do as much as you did then to make $200. Fifteen years ago you had to do more burglaries. See, back then there wasn't a lot of merchandise like there is now. See, you wouldn't have to do three burglaries now because you have VCRs. Back then, you go in a house and get probably a TV. Maybe food. Now you can count on making much more per house for sure: a TV, VCR, microwave, watches, jewelry, and any money that's in the house.

Mark

Mark is the third of five brothers. Two of his brothers are dead and two others are serving time in prison. Mark states that his family has always been considered "white trash," although his father always worked in the oil fields. But because oil booms came and went in West Texas, the family had many "down" years.

Mark was 8 years old when he broke into a house with the encouragement of a male neighbor in his 30s. The target site was three blocks from his own home. Mark asserts:

I had gotten into sniffing paint and glue and I was real high when this guy I was running with wanted me to go in this house and get a stereo for him. It was about midnight and since the people were there and I was so small, I pulled my shoes off and slipped through the back window, opened the back door and got the stereo. That's how I started doing it. I was pretty high.

Mark and his older mentor began burglarizing about one house per week. Mark's job was to enter the dwelling and pass the merchandise out the window to his partner. Another older male neighbor entered the partnership and they began sending Mark down air conditioning vents of drug stores, hardware stores, and restaurants. Where necessary, they'd lower him with ropes. They told Mark what to do and what to get. He averaged about 50 burglaries a year over the next 10 years. When he was 18 he was arrested the first time for burglary. He was placed on probation. Soon afterward he stole a truck while intoxicated on alcohol and drove to Dallas, where he was subsequently caught. They revoked his probation for the earlier arrest and he was sent to prison for 3½ years. Mark was released from prison in August, 1976 and he spent only two days on the streets before he was arrested and later convicted for "cutting some dudes up over at the 'Spot' that was threatening my brother." He returned to prison for 6½ more years after those two days of freedom.

Out again in early 1983 he was free for 102 days until he was arrested for aggravated assault on a police officer. He spent an additional 3½ years in prison on a 10-year sentence. Ninety days after being released from his third incarceration, he was arrested for auto theft. He received a 20-year sentence and served 3½ years. Thus since he was 18 he has spent almost 17 years in prison.

Mark reports always being high when breaking into a target site. His biggest fear is of being shot by an unknown occupant, although he never carried a weapon himself:

Every time I've done a burglary I've been high. Because when I'm not high, I won't do it; because I'm too scared to do anything. I was always drunk or high on marijuana or acrylics; now heroin. It makes me not scared, you know. My biggest fear is being blown away. You know, somebody that's in there and has just been ripped off. They're thinking like me, you know, if I seen a suspicious character pull up to my house and knock on the door, I wouldn't answer the door. I'd wait and if he came in my house I'd shoot him.

Although breaking into a house while high was certainly not unusual, Mark was unusual in that he performed all his burglaries at night, usually after 10:00 p.m. In addition, except for his youthful period working with the two older men, he never planned ahead, saying:

I never really planned a burglary. You know, unless it was a business like a drugstore or a drive-in restaurant. We planned that. But as far as a house went, man, I'd just be cruising and see a house that looked empty and I'd stop and knock on the door. If nobody answered, you know, I'd go inside. Mostly I'm cruising. You see, as far as that goes, man, if I'm real sick, any house would be as good as the other one.

Mark is back in the Texas Department of Corrections, having been sentenced recently for a third charge of theft of a motor vehicle. As his brother told us one day, "Mark will never make it in the free world, he never learned how."

Endnotes

1. After 16 months interviewing and conducting "mock" burglaries with 30 active burglars, we began to develop alert opportunism or, as our informants put it, a criminal mind, ourselves. Although this was extremely disconcerting, we began to view neighborhoods and houses in a different way than we ever had before—in terms of their vulnerability to burglary. Where we had, in the past, seen a nice privacy fence surrounding the backyard of a private residence and either took no particular note of it or possibly thought about how it provided the residents privacy for outdoor activities, we now thought about how well that fence would shield a burglar's activities once inside. Attractive bushes and shrubbery and other landscaping came to be seen in terms of how well or poorly it would hide a burglar.

2. This is a modification of West's (1972) definition of a "serious thief."

3. We wish to acknowledge the assistance of Marcus Felson in labeling this technique, and for his valuable assistance in many other aspects of the research.

4. We usually evaluated two to five previously burglarized sites during a session. However, Session 2 was conducted as early as a week from the time the informant was recruited for the study and we frequently had not had the time to establish sufficient rapport or trust to obtain more than one previously hit site from the informant during this session. Even this was frequently a burglary he or she had been convicted of or had cleared for the police after an arrest for another burglary. Whenever we felt reluctance from an informant during the early sessions, we suggested that he or she initially take us to sites of burglaries for which he or she had no remaining criminal liability: "Let's go look at a place you have burglarized and have already been convicted of or one the police already know about."

5. Although most informants worked with different partners at different times and in different circumstances, we were able to convince at least one of the usual co-offenders to participate in most cases.

6. We are aware of the many problems with validity and reliability associated with using official records. The quantitative study was primarily conducted to assist us in validating the ethnographic data we were collecting. For example, our informants overwhelmingly favored corner houses to houses situated elsewhere on the block. Was this preference real? Or did they tell us what they thought was "correct," based upon jail house bull sessions? The qualitative study suggested that the burglars did indeed prefer corners. We do not believe there is any reason to suggest underreporting underrepresents corner houses, residences close to schools or businesses, and so forth. These variables were the

119

focus of the quantitative study and probably would not be systematically underrepresented in official reports.

7. See Herbert A. Simon (1982) for a more detailed discussion of satisficing.

8. Bennett and Wright (1984) limited the definition of "opportunistic" to offenses precipitated by the sight of a vulnerable target and committed immediately. Furthermore, their sample contained no juveniles, who are thought to be more opportunistic, and was a "deep end" population—most of the sample having five or more previous convictions.

9. We had the advantage of excellent cooperation on the part of local police and were occasionally able to gain access to the informants' criminal records. If the records indicated a drug history and the informants denied drug use, we confronted them with the records. The referring burglar would also occasionally give us information about the subject. Although we did not allow the informants to know the source of our information, we confronted them with a statement such as, "The word on the street is that you use drugs. You can trust us to keep that information confidential. However, we need to know the truth for this study." This gambit worked most of the time. In no case, however, did we confront a burglar in these ways during the first two interviews.

10. George Rengert encountered a similar feeling among burglars in a study in Philadelphia. He described the phenomenon as an "Easter egg hunt" (personal communication, 1988).

11. Burglary is a complex task and cannot be "well-learned." Each burglary target, each environmental situation, is different. Although some aspects of the behavior are similar, each event is unique.

12. There are numerous other reasons that coactors may increase the risks for the burglar, thereby raising the apprehension rate. The presence of coactors in a crime increases the chances that one or more will be indiscreet, talking at the wrong time or in the wrong place, or be seen wearing jewelry taken from the burglary, or inappropriately spending money obtained as a result of the burglary. If arrested, one coactor may snitch on the others in order to reduce his or her own punishment.

13. The materials in this section on desistance and aging out of crime lean heavily on Larry Siegel's *Criminology* (3rd ed., 1989).

14. Carl Klockars (personal communication, 1990) suggests that this is not necessarily true. He states:

Concern for sample content always issues from questions of what it is one proposes to or supposes one is sampling. If one is sampling "burglars" there is no more reason to include more of one type than another. If, however, one is sampling "active" burglars, professional burglars, burglars who are responsible for most burglaries, or accounts of burglary events, then this aspiration *might* lead to a need to target high-rate offenders. It may be that even if certain high rate offenders commit 10 to 20 times more burglaries than the average burglar, the majority of burglaries are, nevertheless, the work of low rate offenders.

References

Åkerström, M. (1983). *Crooks and squares*. Lund, Sweden: Studentlitteratur.

Allport, F. H. (1920). *Journal of Experimental Psychology, 3*.

Barlow, H. D. (1990). *Introduction to criminology* (4th ed.). Boston: Little, Brown.

Beck, A. J. (1989, April). Recidivism of prisoners released in 1983. *Special report.* Washington, DC: Bureau of Justice Statistics.

Bennett, T. (1986). A decision-making approach to opioid addiction. In D. Cornish & R. V. Clarke, (Eds.), *The reasoning criminal*. New York: Springer.

Bennett, T., & Wright, R. (1984). *Burglars on burglary: Prevention and the offender.* Aldershot, UK: Gower.

Blakely, R., & Goldsmith, M. (1976). Criminal redistribution of stolen property: The need for law reform. *Michigan Law Review, 74*, 1511-1613.

Blumstein, A., Cohen, J., & Farrington, D. (1988). Criminal career research: Its value for criminology. *Criminology, 26*, 1-37.

Brantingham, P. J., & Brantingham, P. L. (1978). A theoretical model of crime site selection. In M. D. Krohn & R. L. Akers (Eds.), *Crime, law and sanctions*. Beverly Hills, CA: Sage.

Brantingham, P. J., & Brantingham, P. L. (1981). *Environmental criminology*. Beverly Hills, CA: Sage.

Brown, B. B., & Altman, I. (1981). Territoriality and residential crime: A conceptual framework. In P. J. Brantingham & P. L. Brantingham (Eds.), *Environmental criminology*. Beverly Hills, CA: Sage.

Bureau of Justice Statistics (1988). *BJS data report, 1988.* Washington, DC: United States Department of Justice.

Cameron, M. O. (1964). *The booster and the snitch*. Glencoe, IL: Free Press.

Chaiken, J. M. & Chaiken, M. R. (1982). *Varieties of criminal behavior*. Santa Monica, CA: RAND Corporation.

Chappell, R., & Walsh, M. (1974). Receiving stolen property: The need for systematic inquiry into the fencing process. *Criminology, 11.*

Clarke, R. V., & Cornish, D. (1985). Modeling offenders' decisions: A framework for policy and research. In M. Tonry & N. Morris (Eds.), *Crime and justice: An annual review of research* (4th ed.). Chicago: University of Chicago Press.

Cohen, L. E., & Felson, M. (1979). Social change in crime rates trends: A routine activity approach. *American Sociological Review, 44*, 588-608.

Cohen, L. & Land, K. (1987). Age structure and crime. *American Sociological Review, 52*, 170-183.

Cook, P. J. (1980). Research in criminal deterrence: Laying the groundwork for the second decade. In N. Morris & M. Tonry (Eds.) *Crime and justice: An annual review of research* (Vol. 2). Chicago: University of Chicago Press.

Cook, P. J. (1989). The economics of criminal sanctions. In M. L. Friedlander (Ed.), *Sanctions and rewards in the legal system: A multidisciplinary approach.* Toronto: University of Toronto Press.

Cornish, D. B., & Clarke, R. V. (1986). Situational prevention, displacement of crime and rational choice theory. In K. Heal & G. Laycock (Eds.), *Situational crime prevention: From theory into practice.* London: HMSO

Easterbrook, J. A. (1959). The effect of emotion on cue utilization and the organization of behavior. *Psychological Review, 66,* 183-201.

Farrington, D. (1986). Age and crime. In M. Tonry & D. Farrington (Eds.), *Crime and justice: An annual review of research.* Chicago: University of Chicago Press.

Faupel, C. E. (1987). Heroin use and street crime. *Qualitative Sociology, 10,* 115-131.

Faupel, C. E., & Klockars, C. B. (1987). Drugs-crime connections: Elaborations from the life histories of hard-core heroin addicts. *Social Problems, 340,* 54-68.

Giallombardo, R. (1966). Interviewing in the prison community. *Journal of Criminal Law, Criminology and Police Science, 57,* 395-398.

Glassner, B. & Carpenter, C. (1985). *The feasibility of an ethnographic study of property offenders.* A report prepared for the National Institute of Justice (mimeo).

Glassner, B., Ksander, M., Berg, B., & Johnson, B. (1983). A note of the deterrent effect of juvenile vs. adult jurisdiction. *Social Problems, 31,* 219-221.

Greenberg, D. (1985). Age, crime and social explanation. *American Journal of Sociology, 91,* 1-21.

Hall, J. (1952). *Theft, law and society.* Indianapolis: Bobbs-Merrill.

Hawkins, R., & Alpert, G. P. (1989). *American prison systems: Punishment and justice.* Englewood Cliffs, NJ: Prentice-Hall.

Henry, S. (1978). *The hidden economy.* London: Martin Robertson.

Hirschi, T. (1985). *On the compatibility of rational choice and social control theories of crime.* Paper presented at the Home Office Conference on Criminal Decision Making, Cambridge, England.

Hirschi, T. & Gottfredson, M. (1983). Age and the explanation for crime. *American Journal of Sociology, 89,* 552-584.

Inciardi, J. A. (1979). Heroin use and street crime. *Crime and Delinquency, 25,* 335-346.

Irwin, J. (1972). Participant observation of criminals, In J. Douglas (Ed.), *Research on deviance.* New York: Random House.

Jarbe, T. (1986). State-dependent learning and drug discriminative control of behavior: An overview. *Acta Neurologica Scandinavica, 74,* 37-59.

Johnson, B. D., Goldstein, P. J., & Dudraine, N. S. (1979). What is an addict? Theoretical perspectives and empirical patterns for opiate use. Cited by P. J. Goldstein in J. A. Inciardi (Ed.), *The drugs-crime connection.* Beverly Hills, CA: Sage.

Johnson, B. D., Goldstein, P. J., Preble, E., Schmeidler, J., Lipton, D. S., Spunt, B., & Miller, T. (1985). *Taking care of business: The economics of crime by heroin abusers.* Lexington, MA: Lexington.

Klockars, C. B. (1974). *The professional fence.* New York: Macmillan.

Lab, S. P. (1988). *Crime prevention: Approaches, practices and evaluations.* Cincinnati, OH: Anderson.

Letkemann, P. (1973). *Crime as work.* Englewood Cliffs, NJ: Prentice-Hall.

Lowe, G. (1986). State-dependent learning effects with a combination of alcohol and nicotine. *Psychopharmacology, 89,* 105-107.

Matza, D. (1964). *Delinquency and drift.* New York: John Wiley.

McCall, G. J. (1978). *Observing the law.* New York: Free Press.

Miller, W. B. (1958). Lower-class delinquency as a generating milieu of gang delinquency. *Journal of Social Issues, 14,* 5-19.

National Institute of Justice (1989a). *NIJ reports,* No. 213. Washington, DC: National Institute of Justice.

National Institute of Justice (1989b). *NIJ research in action.* Washington, DC: National Institute of Justice.

Nee, C., & Taylor, M. (1988). Residential burglary in the Republic of Ireland: A situational perspective. *The Howard Journal, 27*(2), 105-116.

Preble, E., & Casey, J. J. (1969). Taking care of business: The heroin user's life on the street. *International Journal of Addictions, 4,* 1-24.

Rengert, G., & Wasilchick, J. (1985). *Suburban burglary: A time and a place for everything.* Springfield, IL: Charles C Thomas.

Rengert, G., & Wasilchick, J. (1989). *Space, time and crime: Ethnographic insights into residential burglary.* A report prepared for the National Institute of Justice (mimeo).

Reppetto, T. G. (1974). *Residential crime.* Cambridge, MA: Ballinger.

Rubenstein, H., Murray, C., Motoyama, T., & Rouse, W. V. (1980). *The link between crime and the built environment: The current state of the knowledge* (Vol. 1). Washington, DC: National Institute of Justice.

Scarr, H. A. (1973). *Patterns of burglary.* Washington, DC: U.S. Government Printing Office.

Shaw, M. E. (1981). *Group dynamics: The psychology of small group behavior* (3rd ed.). New York: McGraw-Hill.

Shover, N. (1971). *Burglary as an occupation.* Doctoral dissertation, University of Illinois. Ann Arbor, MI: University Microfilms.

Siegel, L. (1989). *Criminology* (3rd ed.) St. Paul, MN: West.

Simon, H. A. (Ed.). (1982). *Behavioral economics and business organization* (Vol. 2). Cambridge: MIT University Press.

Steffensmeier, D. (1986). *The fence: In the shadow of two worlds.* Totowa, NJ: Rowman and Littlefield.

Steffensmeier, D., Allen, E. A., Harer, M., & Streifel, C. (November, 1987). *Age and the distribution of crime: Variant or invariant.* Paper presented at the meeting of the American Society of Criminology, Montreal, Canada.

Stimson, G. V., & Oppenheimer, E. (1975). *Heroin addiction and control in Britain.* London: Tavistock.

Sutherland, E. H. (1937). *The professional thief.* Chicago: University of Chicago Press.

Tittle, C. (1988). Two empirical regularities (maybe) in search of an explanation: Commentary on the age/crime debate. *Criminology, 26,* 75-85.

Tittle, C. R., & Logan, C. H. (1973). Sanctions and deviance: Evidence and remaining questions. *Law and Society Review, 7,* 371-392.

Trasler, G. (1987). Cautions for a biological approach to crime. In S. Mednick, T. Moffitt, & S. Stack (Eds.), *The causes of crime: New biological approaches.* Cambridge: Cambridge University Press.

Vold, G., & Bernard, T. J. (1986). *Theoretical criminology* (3rd ed.). New York: Oxford University Press.

Walsh, D. P. (1980). *Break-ins: Burglary from private houses.* London: Constable.

Walsh, M. (1977). *The fence: A new look at the world of property theft.* Westport, CT: Greenwood.

West, W. G. (1978). The short term careers of serious thieves. *Canadian Journal of Criminology, 20,* 169-190.

Wilson, J. Q., & Herrnstein, R. (1985). *Crime and human nature.* New York: Simon and Schuster.

Wolfgang, M., Figlio, R., & Sellin, T. (1972). *Delinquency in a birth cohort.* Chicago: University of Chicago Press.

Wright, R., & Logie, R. H. (1988). How young house burglars choose targets. *The Howard Journal, 27,* (2) 92-103.

Zajonc, R. B. (1965). Social facilitation. *Science, 149,* 269-274.

Zajonc, R. B. (1980). Feeling and thinking: Preferences need no inferences. *American Psychologist, 35,* 151-175.

Zimring, F. E., & Hawkins, G. J. (1973). *Deterrence: The legal threat of crime control.* Chicago: University of Chicago Press.

Author Index

Subject Index

About the Authors

Paul F. Cromwell, Ph.D., is Associate Professor of Sociology and Director of the Criminal Justice Program at the University of Miami. He is the author or coauthor of numerous articles and 12 books, including *Probation and Parole in the Criminal Justice System* (West Publishing) and *Penology: The Evolution of Corrections in America* (West Publishing). He has extensive experience in the criminal justice system, including service as a United States Probation Officer, Chief Juvenile Probation Officer, and Chairman of the Texas Board of Pardons and Paroles.

James N. Olson, Ph.D., is Professor of Psychology and Director of the Division of Behavioral Sciences at the University of Texas—Permian Basin. He is the author of numerous articles in the professional literature and coauthor of *Basic Statistics for the Behavioral Sciences* (Holt, Rinehart and Winston). He has done extensive research on the physiological aspects of drugs and has published his findings in such journals as *Pharmacology, Biochemistry and Behavior, Perception and Psychophysics,* and the *Journal of Drug Education.*

D'Aunn W. Avary, B.A., is a Senior Research Associate in the Division of Behavioral Sciences at the University of Texas—Permian Basin. She is a self-employed consultant specializing in risk management. She is currently engaged in an ethnographic study of the receiving of stolen property and criminal redistribution systems.